ORDINARY
HOUSEWIFE
EXTRA ORDINARY
GOD

CORNELIA MAGNUSSON

WESTBOW
PRESS®
A DIVISION OF THOMAS NELSON
& ZONDERVAN

WestBow Press books may be ordered through
booksellers or by contacting:

WestBow Press
A Division of Thomas Nelson & Zondervan
1663 Liberty Drive
Bloomington, IN 47403
www.westbowpress.com
844-714-3454

ISBN: 978-1-6642-3071-2 (sc)
ISBN: 978-1-6642-3070-5 (e)

Print information available on the last page.

WestBow Press rev. date: 4/30/2021

I dedicate this book to:

The Lord Jesus Christ, my all in all.

My amazing and wonderful husband, who supported me through the whole process of writing, even the difficult passages of our life.

To my precious children, without them I would not have half of the stories of this book.

To my big, beautiful family, as a testimony to the grace of God, for generations to come.

Wonderful stories, beautiful testimonies, powerful miracles. Readers can witness and observe the Hand of God throughout your life. You take them on a journey from the Netherlands to Canada. The descriptive language helps the reader feel they are there with you. Well done!

Pastor Karen-Marie Gariba.

Corine Magnusson is a world changer and has been a mover and shaker for Jesus, wherever she goes, she changes the atmosphere and the lives of people with her infectious love of Jesus that melts the hearts of people. She is a great teacher that brings Biblical truth in her own gentle way. She is compassionate, passionate, a worshipper, and her testimony would change the lives of so many people.

Rev. Pastor Zak Gariba
Lead / Founding Pastor of
Jubilee Celebration Centre
Orillia, Owen Sound, Alliston and Barrie
Ontario.

CONTENTS

PART 3

FOREWORD

When I was employed by Canadian Blood Services, I entertained many blood donors with some of the stories of my life. Being a mother of 10 children and a born-again Christian, having the first health bakery in the area and some 'God moments' throughout my life, I had lots of stories to tell. One lady donor in the city of Newmarket encouraged me to write a book as she found the stories quite interesting and promised she would help me in this venture. It stayed with me, but I did not act upon it.

A couple of years later, our pastor Zak Gariba organized a conference with a motivational speaker: Dr. Keith Johnson

The first thing he asked his audience: "Where are most stories?" It was quiet for a minute or 2 before some answers were offered. "In my heart", "In the library", "In books." "Yes, but where are MOST of them?" he asked again, with the emphasis on most. It was quiet as no one could come up with the answer he was waiting for.

"IN THE GRAVEYARD!" was the answer to his own question.

That was a statement which went straight into my heart and remembered the lady that told me years before to write.

That was 10 years ago. The memories are crisp, and

the Lord helped me to put them on paper. These stories are written for His glory and the furthering of the Kingdom of God. My prayer is, that the reader will be blessed by reading about the miracles that Jesus still performs in ordinary lives.

PART 1

PART 1

1

MY VILLAGE AND FAMILY

The village where I was born and raised was a quaint little place south of Amsterdam. It is called "De Kwakel"

The beginning of this community started already around the year 1000. There is no history on how many people were living in that area at that time. It attracted families in that region because of the marshlands that were overgrown by trees. The farmers cut down the trees and turned that land into fertile farmland. They cut ditches in the land that consisted mainly of peat which created parcels of land for farms. These small waterways were called "*veenstromen*" or peat ditches. Later they built dikes to protect their polder from flooding. *(From Google: A polder: is a low-lying tract of land that forms an artificial hydrological entity, enclosed by embankments known as dikes. The two types of polder are: Land reclaimed from a body of water, such as a lake or the seabed. Flood plains separated from the sea or river by a dike.)*

* *

In 1085 this area came under rule of medieval county of Utrecht, and a provost was their leader. At that time this community had no specific name. In the late Middle Ages, a small centre was formed by a T-junction of 3 streets. They were just small footpaths. These walking trails were also going to some other surrounding villages, some of them hamlets, some of them already had a village status.

'A hamlet in English geography is a community that does not have a church.'

* *

To cross the numerous waterways, they build bridges. These bridges were low at first and made it difficult for boats to go under even though the boats were like flat barges for easy transportation of goods for trade. Since the fourteenth century, there were rules prohibiting the construction of these low-traffic bridges, in order to permit a free passage for shipping. Therefore, higher bridges were built if a fixed connection was needed. *(https://nl.wikipedia. org/wiki/Kwakel)*

As the population grew in the area where my ancestors settled, a bridge was needed to have the communities connect without using a boat as a ferry. One of those higher bridges was constructed over the waterway that was around the polder beside this growing community. The canal was called "*Ringvaart*". It truly was like a ring around the polder that was already having a dike beside the waterway. The timeline for the bridge is unsure but it was built before 1576 according to the history of this hamlet. These bridges were quite rickety hence the name *Quackel* in the old Dutch language, which means shaky. Later it changed to *Quakel* and it is known today as "Kwakel".

Footbridge with anglers by Jan van Gooyen 1651.
https://ilibrariana.wordpress.com/2012/02/27/
een-17e-eeuese-kwakel-in-heemstede-met-schilderfaam/

An Inn and a type of handball court were built beside the bridge in the 2nd half of the 17th Century.

It was impossible for a horse and buggy to cross on such bridges and the need came for drawbridges that were often constructed beside the kwakel-bridges. Some are still to be seen in other villages in Holland.

* *

In the year 1800 a Catholic church was built at the T-junction of these walking paths. Later they became streets and today they are still in the centre of my village. *Boterdijk*, *Kerklaan* and *Kwakelsepad*, translated Butterdyke, Churchlane and Kwakelsepath.

This was the area my grandparents on my father and mothers side chose to move to in the early 1920s from 'Alkemade'. My grandfather Pouw moved and settled in De Kwakel in late October 1922 and my mother's family van der Meer were written in the register on the 17th of January 1925.

The families that settled there were mostly growers of vegetables in the beginning, but many transitioned over to flowers after the war, mainly chrysanthemums on the van der Meer side. My *Opa* Pouw started growing tulip bulbs already in the year 1927. He was quite successful in this venture. According to my aunt, his daughter, he developed 2 new types of tulips. The bulb is of course the money maker as they are shipped and sold all over the world. We like the flowers the best as it is a promise of spring and can only tell by the variety of colors and form that there are different types of tulips bulbs.

* *

When my parents wanted to get married, they first needed to get a place for them to live in. My Opa van der Meer offered my father the shed where they sorted and bound the flowers to be auctioned at *'Veiling Bloemenlust'* which has been renamed as 'Royal FloraHolland' in Aalsmeer in later years. This place is known as the largest flower auction in the world at this time.

My Dad did not think too long about the offer and it was transformed into a small house. It had a tiny kitchen, a living room and a small bedroom behind the kitchen wall. The peaked roof provided some space upstairs for the bedroom of my parents. You could not stand straight up, but since they only slept there, it was adequate for the newlyweds. I believe the total area was about 24 square meters. My sister Nanny was born first there in July 1945, then myself in October 1946 and my sister Marianne in

December 1947. How my Mom managed with 2 active little ones and a baby in that small place is still a wonder.

* *

In 1948 they moved to a new house. The move was made over the canal that is called the 'Ringvaart". Their belongings were put on a barge and Dad pushed a long pole into the canal bottom to move the boat forward. My memory is that my Mom was sitting in the middle with her hand on the baby pram that held my baby sister Marianne, with Nanny and myself close to her side. I am sure there were a couple of boat trips to get everything over.

* *

The new home had 3 bedrooms and a large living room. A kitchen that could hold a table and a room attached to the kitchen that was used for storage and laundry. It had a good-sized garden. A chicken coop was built, and rabbit cages constructed. They were long triangular cages with chicken wire all around and underneath. It also had an enclosed place at the one end for the nighttime or when the weather was nasty. We moved the cages from one place to the next in the garden, so they always had lots of greens to eat. Who needs a lawnmower when you have some rabbits do the job! My father planted blackcurrant bushes around the parameter and an apple tree practically in the middle of the yard. One could go through the backyard to a small canal where my Dad had a rowing boat that would take him to our vegetable patch a small distance away, that was only accessible by boat. Beside the dock he had more berry bushes and a pear tree. That area outside our backyard and close to the water was my favorite place. I studied little bugs that were consuming the bushes' leaves, spiders spinning their webs and watched the frogs trying to catch the flying insects. I was quite satisfied to sit at the water's edge and see the sunrays play on the ripple of the waves.

* *

De Kwakel was a Catholic community. The only family that was not of that faith was the bicycle repairman. Since each family owned at least two bicycles this man was an asset to this village. As a child there were no controversies to worry about or to wonder about different beliefs. My Mom would read Bible stories with many pictures and they made quite an impression on me. One of the stories was about the archangel Michael driving Lucifer out of the heavenlies. He was shown as a big angel with beautiful wings and an armour type suit, with Lucifer and all the fallen angels looking like demons, on the bottom of that drawing. I knew from that time on we had a warrior angel and was not afraid of anything.

* *

First Communion was a big deal for a first grader. That was also true for me. I took the preparation time for this event very seriously. I was going to receive Jesus in my heart and could not wait. Once the big day arrived, all would be ready at home. A special meal was prepared and if aunts and uncles did not have one of their own children take their first Communion, they would be invited along with grand-parents and the Godparents. All that I remember of that day is that I must have pulled away from the busyness at home and walked on a low stone wall in my nice long white dress. With my hands on my heart, I was repeating:

"I have Jesus in my heart, I have Jesus in my heart.".

* *

A couple of years later I would wait until my sister was asleep, crawled out of bed careful not to wake her. I would take a little blue blanket, wrap it around my shoulders, take a plant from a small table so I could stand on it, with a rosary around my wrists. I tried to imitate a picture I had seen of Mary, the mother of Jesus and hoped to become holy like her. Until I got cold or just tired of standing there, I would crawl back in my cozy bed.

* *

Just about every day my Mom would send me to Mass. Often I wondered why I had to be the one and not one of my sisters. Sometimes my younger sister Marianne would accompany me. We would take a long time going home after Mass was done. We would make little circles with twigs and carefully take a spider web that had dewdrops on every strand into the circle. We called them mirrors as we could see tiny reflections of our face in each of the droplets.

* *

Daily Mass was a routine for many of the elderly of De Kwakel. The church had a missal available with the gospel and epistle for every day in the back of that booklet. It was quite thick as it held the writings of the apostles for the whole year. Because I was often in church, I had the words of the Mass in Latin memorized. Every day was the same, which became quite boring. Reading the stories in the back of the missal, which were all out of the New Testament kept me interested. I read well ahead of the intended gospel and epistle for that day.

*   *

Easter 1958 was early in April. If you wanted to stay Catholic, you are expected to go once a year to confession and Communion and that had to be at Easter. Even though as a family we were having Communion every time we attended Mass and went to confession every 14 days, my Mom made sure we all went to confession the day before Easter and then we went with my father to midnight Mass. It always was a feast in the middle of the night at Christmas and Easter. Mom would stay home with the little ones and prepare a breakfast feast for after church. Fancy little knotted buns, real butter, lots of deli meats and cheeses were spread out in the middle of the table. Sweets for on the bread are real Dutch treats. Chocolate sprinkles, colored hail, chocolate spread and ground up candied anise seed are delicious to the Dutch palate. Mom would decorate the butter in the dish and made it look like a flower. Lots of preparations for this important feast were done the previous day. All hands-on-deck to get the house spotless and certain dishes prepared. Mom was convinced that the house had to be clean before Easter.

*   *

Spring cleaning is something that stems from the Passover tradition to make sure that there is no leaven found in any part of the house. As commanded by God before the Hebrews had the meal with unleavened bread the night before leaving Egypt. They are told to celebrate the Passover feast every year, to commemorate the deliverance from the oppressor. They had to, and still is done today, clean out the old leaven before the special meal was shared on the first night of Passover, which is celebrated for 5 days. Maybe because my Mom did the cleaning for a Jewish family in Amsterdam, she picked up on the tradition of a clean house 'before' Easter.

* *

Around noon that Saturday I was told to go to confession and shine all the shoes of the children also Mom and Dad's. Off I went, free for a little bit from household chores. It was a beautiful sunny day, and I did not make haste to be at church and back in record time. I was talking to God while walking along the water's edge of a canal on my way to confession. I said:

"Lord, I will confess all my sins today and leave not one out, then I will not sin anymore."

I really wanted to please God and I thought the only way I could do that would be to live a sinless life. So, I dug up some lies that I had not confessed before: disobediences to Mom, fights with my siblings and more of those transgressions. Afterwards I had to do my penance, which usually was the Lord's prayer three times and a couple of Hail Mary's. Then I walked back into the sunlight. I felt new, fresh and clean. The world I saw was in technicolor, the grass was greener, the sky intense blue and walking back along the same waterway noticed every little creature that lived in the water and at the water's edge. I took my time going home, enjoying the new feeling inside. I told Jesus I would make sure I kept my promise to not sin, until I came home through the back door! Mom was angry that I had taken up so much time for something that usually required about

5 minutes per confession. She threw the shoes to my feet and told me to hurry up. Ah, all my good intentions went out of that back door and I sinned! I was upset at Mom and used the brush on the dried polish with an intensity that made those shoes have quite a shine, once done. Of course, there is a way to stay close to Jesus, to have a personal relationship with the Son of God but I did not get to know that until I was 25 years old. The early-in-life experience is etched in my mind as I am sure Jesus saw my heart and made a way for me to know His love and compassion, His forgiveness and freedom.

2

MY HUSBAND TO BE

We had to move to another location when I was about 10 years old, as my only brother was becoming too old to sleep in the same room with one of his sisters. Our family counted 7 children at that time and more bedrooms were needed.

The little village needed more space also and something like a sub-division was starting to take shape in the polder along the 'Ringvaart'. Two rows of houses were built in an L-shape right beside a farmer's field where cows and sheep were grazing. My Dad and Mom asked for an end unit, which they received. It gave more space outside and an extra window on an otherwise solid wall. A large attic was a bonus. Not only was there room for one double- and a single bed but also lots of storage space.

Since we were blessed with a townhouse at the end of the row, the cows and sheep were only a couple of meters away from our home. One time they broke through the fence. On opening the curtains that morning, the sheep greeted us with their faces right at our front window. The farmer had to be contacted as none of our family members or neighbors were brave enough to get these animals back where they belonged and mend the fence.

*   *

It took a couple of years before more rows of townhouses were added and the subdivision of our little town became a reality. The aircraft company bought a row of these townhouses to rent them out to their employees. Since the distance from our town to the airport was about 10 km, it was ideal for the workers in the aircraft industry. Families from other villages and the city of Amsterdam came to live in 'the Polder'. It was strange to see unfamiliar faces. One of those strangers walked ahead of me to the bus stop. He had curly black hair. While I was waiting for the bus; I glanced at him sideways, and I wondered if he lived in the new row of housing or if he was just a visitor.

A couple of weeks later I had the guts to make conversation with this young man and found out where he lived and his age. He said he was 18 and had moved from Amsterdam in October.

*   *

Who meets the mother-in-law before meeting the husband, without introduction?

A couple of weeks later I was stopped by a lady with the side bags on the back carrier of her bike full of newspapers. She asked for directions to roads that were a couple of km away. Instead of telling her, I asked if she would wait for me to get my bike and I would show her. Together we delivered the papers and after we came back in our neighborhood, she offered me a cup of tea. I did not get her name, but just called her 'Mevrouw', which is not uncommon in Holland. Her little daughter Ria, who was 7 at the time, joined us and we had several tea-biscuits. It was nice to meet some new people and I found out the reason for their move from the big city to such a small town; her husband was a sheet-metal worker for the Aircraft company. I asked if the young man that I met was her son. She told me that she had 3 sons beside Ria. The oldest Michael was 17, a 14-year-old son and John was 12.

"That could not have been one of your children as he told me he was 18" I replied. After I was shown some photographs, I got to know that it was the 2nd son, and he was only 14. As a teenager I was flattered to think that this young boy was trying to make an impression on me.

* *

Winter in the Netherlands is quite mild and of short duration. It does not happen often that it is cold enough to have the canals and lakes freeze over before the end of the year. Sometimes we could skate on the canals before Christmas. That year we had such a winter, to the delight of the children of the village. The '*Ringvaart*' became quite busy with parents and children on skates. Games were organized, and races held. Stands were set up on the side of the canal serving coffee, hot chocolate and some sweets. It was a community gathering on ice. Some little ones were learning to skate either by holding an adult's hand or a wooden chair was put in front of them, and they were pushing it ahead as their ankles were trying to stay straight to be able to make short strides.

* *

One evening I was walking home from visiting family and crossed the bridge over the frozen canal and heard a scraping sound. Immediately I thought: *"Who is skating at this time of night?"* 'Kwakelaars' (villagers were called that) do not skate when it is dark as everyone knows that there could be open water spots that could not be detected when its dark. Once you skate into a hole in the ice it is hard to get out and drowning is a very good possibility. I stood on the bridge for a while and tried to see who this crazy person was. It was too dark for me to see a face and just watched this shadowy figure skating up and down. Not much later I learned that it was the oldest son of my new neighbor. His name was Michael. In time I got to meet him at his home, and we became good friends. I really liked him, more like an older brother which I did not have. We just clicked! That winter we took his little sister skating. It was the first time she was on ice with skates under her feet and we were successful in having her stand on her own and making a few strides.

* *

In the spring I took Ju-Jitsu lessons and Michael was in Judo. We rode our bikes together and enjoyed each other's company. Sometimes after my sister and I had finished the dishes, we played badminton with the brothers M. Michael played soccer in Uithoorn, just a couple of kilometers from our village and I often accompanied him on a Sunday, which was the day that the team played.

* *

As de Kwakel was a Catholic community, dances for young people over 18 were held every 14 days in a hall and the young chaplain that was serving the pastor was the overseer. He had to make sure that there were no brawls, and all attendants were Catholic. The young people did not all live in our village but came from other surrounding towns. Michael became friends with the brothers T from Uithoorn and they invited him to come to these dances. After a couple of weeks some parents complained to the chaplain that there was a non-Catholic boy dancing with their daughters and once the dance was over, he walked some of them home. At that time there was still a lot of segregation between Catholics and Protestants, stemming from the religious wars in the years past.

One day Michael was waiting for me in the front of the house, nonchalantly leaning against a pole with his arms crossed, looking into the large front window. My Dad got upset and closed the curtains.

"Why did you do that Dad?" I asked.

"He is not a Catholic!" was his reply.

It was a deep-seated resentment towards someone of another faith that took many more years to dissipate from my Dad and people in general.

* *

Michael was approached by the chaplain at one of the dances and an appointment was made to meet and talk. After the meeting Michael was found not to be 'dangerous' and was given an entrance card for the dances in the future. Many times, we danced together and also walked home only because we lived in the same neighborhood. On some occasions I asked him to stay close as I had no desire to be in the company of another boy and even though he might have had other ideas for the evening; he stayed by my side. I viewed him as a kind of rescuer on those occasions.

* *

Michael had reached the age that young men were drafted into the Dutch Army, and he showed up at my house in his uniform in March 1964. He had to serve 18 months. One day my Mom said that Michael had come by the house asking for me to cut his hair. Cut his hair? I had never cut anyone's hair. Curling my Mom's hair was the extent of having my hands on someone else's head! When he came over on that weekend, I told him that I had never done this before and not to expect a good job. His answer was that I most likely would do a much better job than the barbers at the Army base. They did the bowl cuts and that was not something he wanted to be seen in. After I had done that first masterpiece, he came over every so many weeks for another cut. Sometimes he had a bit of a bald spot was on the back of his head, but not to worry he said, as his beret would cover it!

* *

In May 1965 he came to the house and asked me on a date. A date! That was quite unusual, and I was intrigued. He rented a car, and we went to Amsterdam which was his birthplace. We had a wonderful Indonesian dinner there and walked around for awhile. It was quite new for me to see the sights and lights of Amsterdam in the evening. I tucked my hand in the crook of his arm and it felt natural and comfortable to walk so close by his side. The drive home was done in a slower pace than the way to the city and not much was said as we knew that our relationship was experiencing a change. Once at home I received my first kiss from him. My mother was already in bed, but Michael asked me if we should wake her and tell her that we were an item. The wise thing to do was to wait until the next day and tell her the news. Mom was quite happy and told me that she had hoped that he would be the one that I would be spending the rest of my life with. A saying that was used to her by my father's oldest sibling when my Mom and Dad were engaged to be married was that if she would marry Piet, she would never experience hunger. She summarized that a bit different and said to me that day:

"Met Michael zal je altijd brood op de plank hebben",

"With Michael you will always have bread on the cutting board".

That meant he would be a good provider. I chuckled and told her that was not hard as he is a baker by trade. We did have a good laugh together!

* *

From that time on I started gathering some nice things for our future together. Sheets, blankets, tablecloths, towels and some nice earthenware dishes were all set aside for a future home. We had no idea where we were going to live once married. My future father-in-law started to check out if there were any apartments available in our village. Since Michael was working for the bakery Berkemeier in Uithoorn, we could also check out that town for some living space. One thing we found out quickly: once you were engaged to be married, you could register at City Hall, and wait for the next apartment or house to become available. There was a long list of potential married couples. WWII was not that far in history and houses were not built in those horrendous years. After the signing of the Peace Agreement in May 1945, it would take some years before life could be called normal again. New subdivisions were taking shape in Uithoorn and my oldest sister and her beau found a townhouse there and got married. Michael and I were not engaged yet and put the thought of getting married off. But that took a turn for the better a month later.

3

CANADA

My Mom had a sister Adriana, her calling name was Sjaan. I was about 3½ years old when she came to visit while Mom was hanging out laundry in the backyard. I still see her running her fingers along the clothesline walking slowly to my Mom. She said something and I saw my Mom sinking down on a chair and crying. Many years later, I realized that she had come to tell her family that she and husband Piet were leaving Holland to make a life in Canada. That was in 1949.

* *

The Netherlands and Canada had signed a post-war immigration agreement for families to relocate and make a living for themselves. Many farmers could not grow anything anymore in Holland as many of the dikes had been destroyed by the German forces, and water covered their land. It also helped Canada to increase their population in rural areas. Almost 100.000 Dutch came to Canada between 1947 and 1954. Almost 80% were farmers and settled in southern

Ontario or Alberta which was also a popular place to move to. (*postwar immigration through Pier 21*)

* *

Tante "Aunt" Sjaan and *Oom* "Uncle" Piet came to Canada with the help of a Catholic organization that would be instrumental in getting them settled. They landed in Quebec City and were picked up by their sponsor who lived in New Brunswick. After they worked for this farmer for 4 years, they made their way to Toronto where they were able to purchase a house. My *tante* Sjaan was experiencing serious health issues and since something like Ontario Health Care was not available until 1966, the bills for hospital stay and doctor's care depleted their savings. They even had to sell their house. I remember that my Mom's siblings were in discussion to have the family move back to the Netherlands. But instead of coming back to live, she came for a visit. That was in June 1965. Even though they had experienced hardship, she was full of praise about their life in Canada.

Many members of the family were present when she arrived at my Opa and Oma van der Meer's house. Michael and I visited a couple of days later. It was wonderful to listen to her stories about a far-away country. She asked me when we were going to get married. I laughed and told her that we first had to get engaged to be even put on the list and then hope that an apartment or townhouse would be available over the next couple of years. She told us that one did not have to wait in Canada. There were plenty of houses and not just townhouses but single dwellings. I am sure my face was getting red as my mind was racing with incredulous thoughts of married life in a little house.

* *

It was time to go home. Michael and I did not walk over the road but over the dike that was along the *Ringvaart.* It was a slow walk over a path that was cut by many pedestrians who chose to walk close to the water. Would we dare to ask *tante* Sjaan if we could go to her and find a starting point in Canada through her and *oom* Piet? We let it rest for a couple of days, but there was no rest in my head. Sleeping peacefully was certainly not the case. Thinking about a start in the unknown was a bit scary but also quite exciting. We did not consider any 'what ifs' and decided to ask *tante* Sjaan if she would allow us to come and stay with her family for a short while. It was like she had expected us to put that all important question to her and had her answer without the usual 'let me think about it' "You are welcome in my home" was her immediate answer. She also told us to get in contact with an agency in Holland for information on which steps to take for immigration into Canada. We said our goodbyes and promises of letter writing as soon as we knew a little bit more of our future move into the unknown.

* *

Michael was released from the Dutch Military on the 15th of August. His Mother and Father planned a camping trip for a couple of days in the province of Brabant. I was invited too, and it was a beautiful time filled with bike rides, hiking and mini golf. This was my very first time sleeping in a tent. Getting used to sleeping on an air mattress and being in a small tent with Mother M and Ria was just a small inconvenience. The tent with the guys was just a stone-throw away from us. We saw so many falling stars while we sat around the campfire as it was the time of the Perseid meteor shower. On August the 19th Michael and I got engaged, under the dark sky with light streaks of the meteor shower above us.

* *

The agency we had to get in contact with had an information session in September of 1965. We had to fill out quite some papers and were told that we could be on the first boat that would go to Montreal. The St. Lawrence River was closed for shipping until half of April because of ice floes in early spring; therefore, a boat with immigrants and tourists could not enter the riverway before that time. Another meeting was in November to present the agents with all the information that was needed to find out if we were eligible to immigrate. Health and education were considered and the fee for the trip was calculated according to the money that was made the year prior to the move to Canada. We had to pay a minimum amount as Michael was in the service and did not get a regular salary, and women at that time received minimum pay. We were accepted for travel and would be sailing to our new country on the 15th of April 1966. A notice was sent to us from the immigration office at the end of November, stating that if we were not married before the end of January 1966, we had to pay for two rooms on the boat. That was a bit of a shock as we were planning to be married in March. We decided to just have a civil wedding in January and then a church wedding in March.

* *

In the Netherlands one cannot just marry in a church as the church pastors are not licensed to officiate at a civil service. Normally a couple would go to City Hall and have the signed copy of proof of marriage and then if they wanted to have a church wedding, go to their church of choice and give their vows to each other before God. We planned for a civil ceremony on January 24. It was a bit of a rush but with the help of my younger sister Marianne I made a nice dress. The ceremony was meaningful for the family M as they did not have any religious affiliations. In their eyes we would be married. They planned a small party in their home. We would continue our regular jobs, Michael as a pastry baker for a bakery in Uithoorn and I was employed by a private medical laboratory in Amstelveen. On Saturdays I worked in a hair salon to make some extra money, washing hair only. We could not live together as my parents said that we were not married before God. Even so we planned to spend all our free time together, enjoying each other's company and talking about our future. Letters were sent to *Tante* Sjaan and *Oom* Piet with the particulars of the journey, and date and time of arrival in Toronto.

* *

On the 24th of January 1966 we became Mr. and Mrs. M junior by law. Within a week after the ceremony my Mom came with the news that she had organized our church wedding for the 13th of April. I was very upset to say the least. She had also made a reservation for a hall with dinner for that day, without consulting us. Her argument was that she did not want me to be pregnant before we left for Canada. I told her that there was something like 'the Pill', but that did not fit in a Catholic upbringing.

* *

Over the previous 2 years I had saved up some beautiful items for when I would set up housekeeping. The sheets, blankets, dinnerware and glasses were to be shipped in a container before we left. The immigration agency had given us the information on how to go about that. Once that was done, the one thing to plan for was our church wedding. I had dreamed of a beautiful long white dress, but money was tight, so I had to settle for a ¾ length gown. I found a satin dress that fitted perfectly on me and our budget. Wearing it made me feel special. Most of our family members were able to make it to our wedding as it was also a goodbye because we were traveling 2 days later. The gifts we received were all monetary for which we were very thankful. A special memory of that day is edged in my mind, dancing the Viennese Waltz with my Dad.

* *

April 15, 1966 had come. My uncle Quirinus drove us to 'Hoek van Holland' where the Maasdam, a ship of the Holland America Line was docked. Some close family members, including our parents and some siblings were saying goodbye to us at the quay. Lots of tears flowed and plenty of hugs were given before we walked onto the gang plank on a ship that would sail us to our new destination. We were on deck and leaning over the rail waving like crazy as the boat pulled away from the harbour. As the people were getting smaller in the distance the dam broke and I sobbed, releasing all the stress from the previous months. My heart was squeezed at the thought that I would not see my parents or siblings for a long time. Once our family became like little stick figures on the quay and the ship was well on its way to the North Sea, we started to explore the layout of the boat. There were two more stops, one in Le Havre, France and the last one in Southampton, England before we would be out on the Atlantic Ocean and we would not see land for a couple of days. We had a tiny room in the bottom of the ship, but that was our sanctuary for 10 days. Finally alone, we could talk freely about our expectations and what lay ahead of us. The boat trip was a wonderful start of our life together.

* *

We had beautiful calm weather for about 6 days, but as we came close to Greenland and Newfoundland, we experienced a good storm. The theatre room on the Maasdam at that time was just a room with chairs placed in front of a screen. We were watching "That Darn Cat". The moment that the cat jumped on dishes stacked high on the counter and came crashing down on the floor, the ship made a roll to portside, and we slid across the floor into each other. It was quite funny if it was not for some of passengers that got hurt. The movie kept on rolling, but many left to find a safer place. The tables and chairs in the dining room were chained to the floor and no soup was served. The tables had a ridge around the edge so dinnerware would not slide off.

* *

The ship had received stabilizer fins in 1955, to minimize the 'pitch and roll'. (*www.ssmaritime.com Remembering the classic liners of yesteryear*) It became more comfortable for the passengers after that improvement. Still it was not as good as the cruise ships of today, and many people became sick. One passenger lost his dentures overboard and a call was made for some financial help to get new ones in Canada. It was then that Michael noticed that the money he had put in the inside pocket of his blazer, was not there anymore. Panic hit us! Where could it be? We were told not to keep valuables in our room, as there was no safe to lock away important items. Still, we did a thorough search through our belongings in our cabin, but Michael knew that it had never been anywhere else but in that inside pocket. Coming to the realization that we had been robbed, dampened our spirits. What now? How were we going to set up housekeeping in an empty house? Some passengers had become friends on our journey, they suggested that there should be a collection for us, but that was not to be. Thankfully, we were going to be with my aunt and hoped for some wisdom on this penniless situation.

* *

On day 9 we cruised through the St Lawrence River on our way to Old Quebec City. It was exhilarating for this young married couple to be out on deck to see the river's edge. Warm clothing was a must as snow was still plentiful on the hills in the distance. We reached our first stop in Canada late afternoon and quite a few tourists or immigrants disembarked. For the last evening aboard the Maasdam the staff had organized a farewell party. It was a wonderful time with dancing and gifts for some who won certain competitions. One of those challenges was dancing the limbo. My husband was very athletic as he played many sports back in Holland, an excellent swimmer, soccer player and judo competitor. He participated that night in dancing the limbo. To my amazement he won that competition, while the ship sailed us to Montreal. We arrived there early on the 25th of April 1966.

* *

The only meal we were served was breakfast. The dining room was cleared of tables and chairs and all the suitcases were brought up from the hold in the bottom of the boat. We had to find our suitcases which were marked according to cabin numbers. The passengers were told to make their way with all their belongings to the exit to disembark. Michael might have been very athletic but had not used his leg muscles too much over the last half year as we were preparing to emigrate. The muscles in his thighs were extremely tender. He struggled to walk down the gangplank with 2 of our suitcases; I followed him with the 3rd. No wheels on suitcases at that time. If he had not been in so much pain, I would have laughed out loud as it was quite comical to see him walk with bended legs and the suitcases almost dragging over the ground. We arrived at the Montreal train station around noon and had to wait for the train to Toronto. That train was scheduled to leave at 6 pm and arrive in Toronto at 12 midnight. We had no money, no lunch and no supper. A reverend who had heard about our plight had given us $2.00 to buy some sandwiches. Michael was in pain; we were hungry and most irritable. That sandwich was just an appetizer and there was no meal to follow up. We kept it together and were happy to arrive at the Toronto station where my uncle Piet was waiting to take us to his home. It was a happy reunion with my *tante* Sjaan. When she heard that we had nothing substantial to eat since we left the ship, she prepared us some fried eggs on dark bread. It tasted like a banquet in the middle of the night. We had thankful hearts and full tummies on our first night on Canadian soil.

* *

We stayed with my *tante* Sjaan until the first long weekend in May. We were directed to visit the Canadian Consulate, which we did immediately. We had my cousin who was not quite a teenager to interpret for us. He could understand Dutch but not speak it fluently, yet he was a great help as the school English we spoke did not quite cut it in normal speech. We got registered and filled out forms to receive our Social Insurance Number. We also received $39.00. Then we were shown a list of bakery businesses where Michael could apply for a job. He chose a Dutch bakery and was accepted on the spot. He started his new job the week after. Michael was told that he would not be working in Toronto for the summer but at a tourist area called Innisfil. There the boss rented a cottage for us on St Johns road. Our first little home and on our own! It was sparsely furnished but had everything one needed to set up housekeeping.

* *

My husband worked long hours from 1 in the morning until 2 sometimes even 4 in the afternoon. I worked in the bakery from 8 am until Michael was done. Still we found time to cruise around in our little 2-seater, a Nash. Barrie was the biggest town in the area, and we became quite familiar with the plaza where they had a laundromat. I am sure my eyes were like saucers the first time I visited that business. There was nothing like that in the Netherlands. We explored the villages around Barrie and fell in love with the landscape. After the summer was over, we found a little house on the corner of Bayfield street, which at that time was a dirt road to Elmvale, and highway 400. Michael found it hard to drive up and down from Barrie to downtown

Toronto every day and found a new job in Richmond Hill. The new boss did not like him to drive from where we lived to his bakery and told my husband to move closer to his business. We settled in Thornhill and I found a job in the lab at the York Central Hospital.

* *

On the boat we became friends with a couple that also stayed in the Toronto area. We made an occasional visit and found out that they were moving back to Europe as his uncle had died and left a bar in Belgium in his will to our friend. We were offered to buy the furniture that they had brought over from Holland. What a provision for a couple that had nothing to their name. In the summer we had already bought the necessary items for kitchen and bath, but comfortable furniture was the last thing on our minds. By the time our first child was to be born we were living in a farmhouse on Yonge Street north of Richmond Hill.

4

A CHANGE FOR THE BETTER

In 1971 we started a health food bakery in Aurora ON and called it Genuine Health Bakery. Baking days were on Sunday and Wednesday. Around 6 am we came to the production site and did not leave until around 4 pm the next day. Most of the time we had about 1000 loaves of bread to bake besides muffins, danishes and other baked goods to fill the orders. Some deliveries to Aurora, Newmarket and Richmond Hill we did ourselves and this made for long and tiring days. Most of the deliveries in Toronto were done by some friends of friends, and we were always relieved that we received payment! After a couple of weeks, we learned they could be trusted; but we did have our misgivings in the beginning of our venture. Our two sons, Zach 3, and Arjan 1 were with us all the time. There was enough room for them to play in the bakery, create things with dough and sleep at appropriate times on the flour bags which we made into safe little beds.

* *

We were about 2 months into our new business when I got a urinary tract infection. It was quite bad as a high fever had started and I experienced a lot of pain. I phoned my doctor who also was our friend, Dr. Roger W. He told me to send a urine specimen to the Lab in Aurora right away, so he would receive the results that same day. When I placed the bottle in front of the lab-assistant, she thought it was blood. I was surprised to get a call from my doctor within the hour, he wanted to see me right away to put me on an antibiotic. I did not have the car until the work and deliveries were done, so no visit to the doctor that day. Michael wanted me to go home and rest and take some meds for the fever. The baking was only half done and since he could not do it alone; he phoned his Mom and Dad to help him. As soon as they arrived, Mom M drove me home with the children and returned to the bakery to get the packing done, which was primarily my job. After some rest and medication, the fever went down somewhat, and I felt well enough to phone Yoka. She was our closest friend at that time and since I could not call my Mom, I reached out to her for some sympathy. She did not seem to listen to me. No inquiries how I was doing, as she was too excited about an experience that she and her husband had gone through, earlier that week. She babbled on about an something that happened to them "in the spirit". I had no clue what she was talking about, and really was not interested. The Lord this and God that; went in one ear and out the other. She shared that they were having a new language and called it 'speaking in tongues' and that stayed with me. I was quiet and at one point she stopped talking and then began to ask me why I had called her.

"I am sick Yoka"

I went on to tell her that Michael was not done with the baking yet and Mom and Dad M were helping him. A doctor's appointment was scheduled for next day as I had a urinary tract infection.

"We will pray for you tonight" was her answer.

"Yah, sure Yoka...".

I had expected her to comfort me with something other than prayer but did not know 'what' I wanted to hear. I missed my own Mom. The next day after 4 pm, I drove myself to the Dr's office. He checked me out and prescribed an anti-biotic and sent me on my way. Well, I did not have any money for that medication, as we would not receive any payment until Friday, after all the baked goods were delivered.

* *

Something happened the next morning that made me think that I was pregnant. A very nauseous feeling made me hold my stomach. First, I thought it might be the illness, but deep down I knew it was something wonderful! I phoned my doctor with my suspicion and he warned me about the strong meds he had prescribed.

"Don't take any more until I have given you a check-up this afternoon, just to be on the sure side."

I did not dare say that I had not even bought the meds. Fighting traffic on a Friday afternoon was not something I wanted to do when not feeling well. But it was my doctor's orders. Around 2 o'clock I was expected at the office and hoped I would not have to stop on the side of the road as the nausea kept coming in waves. I was halfway there and started to feel good, no more pain in my lower abdomen and the fever left me. Still nauseous, but I was sure that was not because of the infection.

By the time I saw Dr. Roger I was all smiles. He asked

for another urine sample and I was surprised that it was so clear. I could not believe my eyes when I handed it over to him. He tested it with one of those dip sticks and no bacteria were detected. He accredited the few pills I had presumably taken for the clear urine, and I did not dare say otherwise. The Lord had healed me instantly, although I did not realize it until much later after I had made a commitment to Him, as I had never heard of a healing without medications. Once I learned of the grace of God and His healing power through the cross, the Lord brought me back to this experience. The doctor said that my womb was tilted and that there was a very slim chance I would be able get pregnant. He sent the urine specimen to the lab for a pregnancy test. Sure enough, a couple of days later the lab confirmed that I was with child and I was quite excited. We hoped for a girl!

All that my friend Yoka had shared disappeared in the background.

* *

Later that week she phoned me and invited me to come to one of the meetings they had. I had forgotten about their new experience and wanted to share my excitement about a new baby with her, so agreed to make the trip from Richmond Hill to their church in Oakville. Before that day I had never stepped into another church other than a Catholic one and was a little nervous. Sitting in the back, I checked things out with a critical eye. It was quite an event for me. I was skeptical of everything that was said and done, and in my heart I poked fun at certain procedures. I heard someone 'speak in tongues' and he said among other words: "Mama Mia" and laughed, saying to myself: "That is Italian!"

* *

After the service, I was invited to go to my friend's place have coffee and some snacks before going back home as I still had a good hour of travel ahead of me. Yoka's husband had invited their elder to come over to answer any questions that they themselves could not answer, if I had any to ask. I had no questions, but the conversation led in the direction of faith and I had my set of beliefs that I felt were solid and no change was necessary in my life. I defended the Catholic Church to the best of my ability. It was not that they attacked that belief system, it was in 'my mind' that they did. They just pointed to my own heart and the need of forgiveness no matter how good I felt that I had lived. I never forgot the question that was asked of me:

"If you would die tonight, are you certain that you will go to heaven?"

Not that I had plans to leave this earth or to give in to their pressure, but I had to be honest and answered with a negative.

"Would you like to make sure?"

The next inquiry came quickly, and it took some thought on my part.

"Yes" I said.

We knelt and a prayer was said. I had no idea how to pray myself but told them I did not need help. No humbleness there!

* *

Before I went home, they prayed for me to be safe on the road. When I hugged Yoka and said goodbye, she encouraged me to do one thing:

"Corine, talk to Jesus like a friend."

On my way home I did say:

"OK I need to talk to You just like a friend, but don't really know how, I will just say The Lord's Prayer".

Somehow, I knew I should not say a Hail Mary. I spoke the words very slowly and really tried to say them to the Lord, but when I came to *"Forgive my trespasses, as I forgive those that trespassed against me"* I had to stop! There were so many hurts in my heart from the past that were mostly family hurts. Number one on my long list of those I had to forgive was my Mom. Then one by one I forgave the persons that came to my mind. After that I asked God to forgive me, as I knew well that I had not lived up to His standards. By the time I drove past the Ford car manufacturer on the QEW, I was feeling so free and light that my heart was flying. It brought me back to my experience when I was about 11 years old.

I had a new beginning!!

* *

From there on it was a slow exit from the Catholic into the Pentecostal Church as I had fond memories and some God-moments when I was a little child. In my mind I was throwing that all away if I would leave the Catholic Church. Later I realized that it was not an end, but an extension of my experiences in my early childhood. The Bible truth became the solid base for my spiritual future.

5

DABBLING IN THE OCCULT

There was an experience in my early life in Canada that the Lord pointed the finger to once I started to learn about past involvements in ungodly practices.

My sister Sjaantje died in a terrible car accident, she was only 19 years old and engaged to be married. 3 out of the 4 occupants of that car were killed. I could not go to Holland for the funeral as we did not have money for the airfare and even if I had enough or could borrow the amount, I was 8 months with our second child. I inquired about traveling overseas at the end of a pregnancy. The airlines would not allow it. That was a very, very sore spot in my heart.

* *

I had already dabbled into the 'unknown' through books and talks with some interesting people. I was very much into Astrology and was plotting my friend's future on charts and was liked for my knowledge in this area. I wanted to buy some other books on the subject to learn more, but my husband would not allow it. That of course did not stop me from continuing to seek out experiences in the psychic realm. I wanted to experience something 'supernatural'.

One evening in February 1970, when Michael was working his second job as a taxi-driver, I decided that even if I could not go to Sjaantje's funeral, I would seek to contact her through the psychic realm, to ease my pain. Positioning myself to receive from the supernatural, I concentrated on the unknown in a kind of meditative exercise. After a little while, a wind went through the room that made my hair move and I felt satisfied that I had contacted another realm. It did not go any further than that, but I liked that something happened beyond my own doing.

* *

Even though I was going to church and was singing in the choir, I did not feel I was doing anything wrong by seeking out the spiritual realm. I had never heard that it was forbidden by the Catholic Church but learned later that it condemns all forms of divination, magic or sorcery and occult powers.

In March that year I gave birth to our second boy. I never thought I would have the same love for a second baby as I had for our oldest son, but to my amazement love just multiplied naturally! It made my heart grow bigger and I was so thankful for these gifts from heaven. I did go through a couple of days of feeling depressed and could not stop crying. In those early years one spent about 5 to 7 days in the hospital, and it gave me enough time to get a hold of myself. I did not stop mourning for the loss of a younger sister but could give it a place in my heart.

* *

Two events in succession had me turn my eyes inward and take inventory of what was going on in and around me. The first one was in our bedroom as I was changing the bed sheets. As a good Dutch girl, I hung the blankets out over the windowsill to air out. The old farmhouse we lived in had windows that were close to the floor, and no screens. Zach, who was about 16 months old was leaning over the blankets looking out. I saw it in the corner of my eye and wanted to give him a stern warning to get away from there. Before my words came out of my mouth an almost audible voice said: "Give him a push". I grabbed Sven and held him close with the most horrible feeling inside my belly. How could I have even had a thought like that! I loved my boy to bits, and this was in my head? I tried to shake it off, but it took quite some time before it was no longer in the forefront of my mind. It lurked somewhere though and made me feel guilty and ashamed.

* *

A couple of weeks later I was doing laundry. The washing machine did not have an automatic softener dispenser and I had to listen for the rinse cycle for me to add the softener. I was nursing my little boy when I heard the rinse water entering the tub and walked over with the baby in my arms. I opened the lid and as I was pouring the softener liquid the same kind of half audible voice commanded: "Throw him in!" I threw the lid down and ran to the living room. That scared me big time and made me wonder what kind of mother I was. How can I even think of these terrible acts! I grabbed Zach from the floor where he was playing, took him on my knee with one arm and held my boys close for a long time. Rocking back and forth I felt the sting of guilt in my heart.

Where did that voice come from? Why was I hearing these horrible commands?

*   *

My husband and I never wanted to live in an apartment building. We sat on the steps of the local newspaper business to be the first ones to grab the weekly paper and search out the ads for houses to rent. The one for rent was on a good-sized property with trees on both sides of the long driveway. I was about 5 months pregnant with our first child when we moved in. From the neighbors we learned that it was a Century old house. Sometime later they told us a murder had taken place in the basement. With the knowledge of that news I was determined never to go down there again. Today I know that one can be influenced by a territorial spirit, a demon that has the right through sin to take possession of a certain area. Looking back on the experiences I had with my infant sons, I had opened the door of my heart to the devil through the occult. This territorial spirit had the right to be in that house through an act of murder by its owner, and even if I had not committed that grievous sin, it would hold me in the clutches of guilt and shame, through the thoughts that were placed in my mind.

*   *

After my "new life experience" some 2 years later and through reading the Bible, the Lord showed me in His word that He was against those that were dabbling in the psychic realm. It made me read books that were written by Christians on the subject. One book that made a big impression on me is: 'From Witchcraft to Christ' by Doreen Irvine. If there was a speaker on this subject, I wanted to hear it. I decided to cut out of my life anything that was remotely connected to the occult and burn the books I had in possession, renouncing any connection with that realm. I also wanted to be led and guided by the Holy Spirit and not any spirit. It was a humbling but empowering experience. I have no fear of the works of darkness but am strong in the knowledge that the Blood of Jesus cleanses all unrighteousness. It makes for the most powerful weapon in our Christian arsenal. I was totally set free at a Full Gospel Business Meeting in Toronto through laughter! That was truly a refreshing experience.

Let no one be found among you who sacrifices their son or daughter in the fire, who practices divination or sorcery, interprets omens, engages in witchcraft, [11] or casts spells, or who is a medium or spiritist or who consults the dead. [12] Anyone who does these things is detestable to the LORD; because of these same detestable practices the LORD your God will drive out those nations before you. Deuteronomy 18:10-12 KJV

There is always a fight for good against evil, even within us. I belong to the winning team; there is no loss now or in the future with Jesus Christ.

6

SMALL BEGINNINGS

After my commitment to God on the way home from Oakville, I had no desire to go anywhere else than the Catholic Church. I sang in the choir and had my friends there. Yoka did not phone me for about 14 days after my visit to their house. When she did, she was surprised to hear my excitement about my conversion. I was invited to come to a mid-week prayer meeting in Bramalea. She knew that we were working on Sundays so she hoped I would be able to come on Wednesdays. I told her that was not possible as we also had a baking day on Wednesday that continued until Thursday afternoon.

I did go to some gospel businessmen meetings. They were held in Toronto every month on a Saturday morning. To worship together with about a thousand believers was just incredible and I enjoyed it very much. The invited speakers were not only interesting to listen to but challenged my Catholic belief. One such speaker was a former Catholic priest who stepped away from the priesthood after the Lord had filled him with the Holy Spirit and while he did his vespers, he spoke in a heavenly language. He was commanded to just say the prescribed prayers. He searched the Bible and told his superiors that it was scriptural what he did. He was forbidden to pray the heavenly language God had given him. He then felt compelled to say goodbye to Catholicism. That was an eye opener for me, and I wanted the infilling of the Holy Spirit. Another month went by and I earnestly desired for the Holy Spirit to give me the gift of speaking in tongues. Judson Cornwall was the invited preacher and I hung onto every word he said. After the meeting he invited the ones that needed salvation to go to one room and the ones that had a desire to be filled with the Spirit, to go to another room. I made a beeline to the 'other' room. We were encouraged to just praise the Lord. Mr. Cornwall laid hands on a couple of worshippers before he came to me. Once those hands touched my head, I started laughing and could not stop. It was very freeing. He then took my hands and laid them on the heads of other believers.

He said: "Now go and do the same."

Some started speaking in tongues immediately; others fell on the ground as they were touched by God. I was amazed at was what was happening around me, still laughing as I moved. I wanted to speak in tongues, that was my greatest desire at that moment, but that did not happen that day.

* *

The next special meetings at the church in Oakville were not long after that special Saturday which I relived repeatedly. I had not stopped asking the Lord for that special gift of tongues and I was speaking a heavenly language in my dreams, but not yet audibly. On one of those nights in Oakville I received what I had desired since the ex-priest in Toronto gave his testimony. I was in heaven! Something of

God took place within me. Receiving the Holy Spirit just like the apostles on Pentecost gave me great joy. From that time on I desired to fellowship with those that were likeminded.

* *

By the grace of God, they changed the mid-week prayer meeting to Thursdays, so as to create an opportunity for me to attend. I asked my husband if he wanted to come with me, and to my surprise he immediately agreed. Going to Bramalea from Richmond Hill after 36-hour workday was a challenge, but Michael drove up and I would drive back home. I snoozed while my husband was driving the 45-minute trip there. The meeting was held in the basement with a woodstove in the corner that kept it nice and toasty. Michael sat close to the fire, so it was no surprise that he fell asleep almost immediately. That was the norm for about 2 months. As my husband was sleeping, those that were present prayed over him for the Lord to touch his heart and give him salvation. One Thursday evening just before Easter, I was having my eyes closed and praising the Lord, someone touched my shoulder and told to open my eyes and be amazed. There was Michael on his knees with his arms raised to the Lord.

My joy was full: just filled with the Holy Spirit, expecting our third baby and my husband saved. My heart overflowed with thanksgiving!

* *

Shortly thereafter we were invited to join a little fellowship in Cooksville in the west end of Toronto. Pastor and Mrs. Hardy became our spiritual parents. There was a lot of love between their family and ours. Their daughter was about the same age as me and in time little ones were added to her family as well as ours.

It was a time of learning and taking in all that the Lord has for His children. We were taught about the gifts of the Holy Spirit and were excited to see them operating in our lives. Often, we had prayers for healing as we are in these mortal bodies fighting off colds, flu or disease. I laid hands on my own growing tummy almost daily, praying for a healthy baby. We desired to have a girl beside our 2 boys, but we could only hope. When I was 8 months pregnant, Michael and I were baptized in the Credit River.

* *

Our new baby was born in September 1972. We were overjoyed that it was a little girl, we called her Stephanie. A tiny little one and a wish fulfilled. While still in the hospital, I was given an X-ray on my lungs. I do not know why, but my doctor found it necessary to check this out. A couple of days later I was to come to his office and was given the news that there were spots on my lungs. He immediately made an appointment for me to see a specialist in Toronto. At that time, you did not have to wait 6 to 9 months for an appointment. I was scheduled to see him about 2 months later.

In the meantime, I went for prayer, looking to Jesus for healing. He had healed me so gloriously before my commitment to him and I expected His touch on my lungs. As I was anointed with oil and prayed for, I felt as if I was inhaling menthol; it was strong but had no smell. It was going deep in my lungs and I knew Jesus had healed me.

* *

The day to see the specialist had arrived and I made my way to his office. It was on the 4rth floor of this building. I stood waiting for the elevator along with people on crutches and 2 patients in wheelchairs. More patients were arriving to go up and I decided to take the stairs so I would not be late for my appointment. The specialist asked me quite a few questions about my breathing, listened to my lungs and asked how many flights of stairs I could walk up without being out of breath. I told him that I 'ran' up the stairs to his office without any problems.

"You did? And well out of breath?" he asked.

"Not really" I replied: "Just a faster heartbeat, but not out of breath."

He looked at me like he did not believe me and sent me for more tests to see how much volume I had in my lungs and ordered more X-rays. I do not recall what the results were for the X-rays, but the tests for volume and ability to breathe deeply without coughing were negative for any problems. The specialist signed me off and declared my lungs clear.

* *

Our oldest son had bronchitis from the time that he was 3 months old and was prescribed antibiotics many times to fight the infection. He was 4 years old when he was hanging in a chair, his breathing very laboured, looking pale with dark circles under his eyes.

"Mommy....I....am....so....tired" he would say, taking a breath between each word.

All I could do was hold him as I was feeling so helpless. I said to my husband:

"This Sunday we are going to have him prayed over. This cannot go on, look at him!"

After the morning service we went up for prayer. Mrs. Hardy took me by the arm and said:

"Come and join me, let the men pray over your boy."

I took my baby Stephanie and Arjan to a room adjacent to the auditorium. There her and I prayed together for healing, while the men laid hands on Zach. After a while we went and joined the rest of the group and Zach came running up to me and said:

"Mommy, I almost cried," which in turn made me cry!!

From that time on he had no more breathing problems. He was totally healed from bronchitis.

What a gracious Father we have, looking after our young family and through these wonderful healings, instilling in me a trust and faith.

7

TRIP TO BC, DELIVERANCE FOLLOWED

About 4 years after Michael and I had made the choice to follow Jesus, we got a visit from some friends who lived in BC. We had not seen them for quite some time and the conversation was mainly some questions and answers about the daily routines just to get reacquainted. They knew that we had another baby, Joshua and they wanted to meet him. Soon Michael and I were talking about our walk in the Lord. We saw that they were interested in what we said. We got the message to their hearts and after a while they came to church one Sunday evening.

After the service, an invitation was given for salvation and our friends went forward. They had counted the cost and made the decision to follow Christ. Pastor Hardy laid hands on them and the miracle of a sinners turning saints was a fact. The wife of our friends needed some deliverance and Mrs. Hardy ushered me and my 2-month-old baby Joshua into another room where we prayed for her freedom. She felt it was better to be away from a deliverance prayer with such a little one and started pleading the Blood of Jesus over us for protection.

* *

Right from the start of our Christian walk we were introduced into what kind of ministries were available for those that are called according to His purposes: salvation, healing, prophecy and deliverance, just to name a few. Our pastor at that time made us aware of certain Christian conferences that would be helpful for us to get a good foundation in all that God had for us according to the scriptures.

* *

Many of us, who start out on the narrow way following Jesus, are too weak to be among those that are friends in the world. As we look to the life of Paul in Acts, to be separated for a time from the life we used to live, to be grounded in the Word and be strengthened in the ways of Christ, is the wisest choice we can make. And thus, our friends decided to stay in the neighbourhood. To be gainfully employed the husband started to work with Michael in the Health Food Bakery.

After a couple of weeks, the couple wanted to get their belongings from their old place in BC and asked if I would be willing to go with the wife, to be her companion and strength to meet with their old neighbors that were at one time close friends. Our 3-month-old Joshua was coming along, and I needed to prepare to have our 3 older children looked after, for about a week to 10 days.

* *

Once everything was in place for this Mom to leave, we set out in our Datsun 610 for a long trip to the west. My dear friend was at peace all the days that we were traveling, and we thanked God for His goodness. Coming to the base of the Rocky Mountains was quite an experience for me, the views were breathtaking. It was not long after, that the shadows started to grow longer, and the sun was quick to be out sight by these mountain tops to the west, as we were going deeper into the interior. It was time to find a little motel to eat and rest and bathe my little Joshua. While I was changing his diaper, I noticed that he was having a problem with his breathing.

Bronchitis was an illness that our oldest son had, starting at the 3-month mark and I battled it too when I was a baby until around 9 years of age. Our family doctor said that I would grow out of it and that is exactly what happened.

When your baby is only 3 months of age and has bronchitis, you take him right away to a doctor as little ones do not have the strength to keep breathing through the obstruction in their bronchial tubes. And here we were in the Rockies far away from any medical facility. The humidity from the mist that was hanging in between the mountains and falling temperatures made it quite uncomfortable. I wished that there was a fireplace or a baseboard heater we could fire up that would expel the moisture. I knew how important dryer and warmer air was to my baby. Even the bed sheets felt damp and cold. As I held Joshua close, kissing his forehead, feeling the heat on my lips knew that he had started a fever. My friend and I prayed together for his health, to ease the breathing and stop the fever. Still, I wanted to go and find a doctor as I was in fear for my baby's life. My companion encouraged me to trust the Lord, a baby herself in Christ and she showed more maturity than me at that moment!

* *

There was a great battle going on in my head, the one side of me said:

"Trust the Lord", the other half was giving me all kinds of scenarios in the negative:

"That baby is not going to make it".

"Trust the Lord"

"It will be your fault; you are not providing the necessities of life to little Joshua".

"You prayed, trust the Lord!"

"He is getting hotter; he needs medical attention!"

"I am the Lord, trust me."

The dialog went on for quite some time, I nursed Joshua and gave in to my Lord and Saviour's voice and rebuked the voice that steals peace and causes fear.

"Lord, I trust your promise."

Joshua was in the crook of my arm close to my heart, and I drifted off to sleep. When I woke up halfway through the night, Joshua's fever was gone, and he was breathing easy. Thankfulness flooded my soul; the trial was behind me but the significance of listening to God's voice stayed in my heart. We had a good breakfast and were soon back in the car for the last leg of the journey.

* *

Certain roads leading to our destination, were like narrow paths, with the mountain wall on our left and the 40 to 50 feet deep valleys immediately on our right, with butterflies in my stomach as I looked to my right, we slowly climbed higher and higher. Those paths were for cattle to get them to from one mountainous pasture to the next, not really for cars to drive on. At one point around a bend was a big bull with huge horns in the middle of the road.

I was given a warning of the danger as my friend was more aware of the power of these animals than I. We had come to a stop about 30 feet away from this bull that was not going to move, no matter how often we tooted our horn or yelled out of the window. There we sat and prayed for wisdom.

After a couple of minutes I felt an urging from the Holy Spirit, opened the door and stood beside the car. Pointing my finger to the beast I said in a loud voice:

"Move in the name of Jesus!"

Lo and behold, he jumped sideways and went out of the way. We rejoiced and I had a bit of the giggles because of what we had just witnessed. It was one of many "God moments" on that trip.

We came to our destination. It was not much more than a rough cabin. My dear friend entered, and I followed right behind her only to find the place ransacked. She was quite disappointed, went through some stuff and she said with a strong voice:

"There is nothing here worth taking with me!"

With that statement she put a big exclamation mark behind her past.

* *

She wanted to visit the neighbors that lived just a bit further away before we would start our return to Ontario. These people had a nice house and a hobby farm. She wanted to say goodbye to that family as she would not be back in that area for a long time. We were welcomed with open arms and when my companion let them know that she and her husband had committed their lives to Christ, there was great rejoicing as they loved the Lord and had been praying for their neighbors for many years. An invitation was made to stay at their house for a couple of nights, which we accepted with grateful hearts. News went around at the speed of lightning that their acquaintance was back for a visit and the next evening the place was full of old friends. It was a wonderful experience. Testimonies were shared, prayers given to those in need and questions asked and answered.

One couple wanted to have a well drilled on their property. They shared that the company would water-witch to pinpoint where the water could be found.

That was my chance to tell them about my experience in the occult before I came to Christ. If water-witching was based on scientific proof, anyone could do it, but those in the dark arts will tell you that only certain people have the ability, which had to do with the connection they have with Satan's kingdom. It was just another scheme to lure the unsuspected into occult practises. I strongly suggested we just pray and ask the Lord for the right place to drill. They were going to take it into consideration. Once we were back home in Ontario, I inquired if my friend had any news about the choice that the couple made to get water. It was hard to hear that they had a company water-witch and spend approximately $ 2000.00 for them to drill, but they could not find water.

* *

The trip out West gave me a wonderful feeling of being in God's protective hand. His guiding and leading and allowing to me to minister outside our home was very new to me. To see my sister-in-the-Lord so strong in her faith in such a short time was such a blessing. We both learned a lot through that trip, from God and each other.

Although she had experienced no great disturbances in her spirit while we traveled, I was made aware that she was still being harassed by the enemy. She diligently read scriptures and prayed. We had faith that one day she would not be bothered anymore. Deep in my heart I was putting a question to the Lord about this situation, why is this process taking so long?

* *

I had read the book 'From Witchcraft to Christ' by Doreen Irvine, who was a queen of the witches in England. She came to the Lord and had a dramatic release of the devil's clutches, but it took almost half a year after her conversion before she was totally free. Doreen was a queen of the witches and my friend might have been in some dark places but was certainly not in the hierarchy of Satan's helpers. Answers from God do not come on our mandate. I had to leave all my questions at the foot of the cross and keep praying for her freedom.

One day she came for a visit and some fellowship. At one point she was standing in the kitchen and I saw her grasp the counter's edge, her face was twitching, and her eyes became dark. I was led by compassion and determination; I pointed my finger:

"Enough devil, out you come in the name of Jesus, no more torture, no place for you now or ever again."

The enemy was not giving up without a fight and I was threatened but knew who I was in Christ.

"Oh, no you are not going to hurt me, I belong to Jesus Christ, I am washed in His blood, and you are going to leave now!"

I went to the front door and opened it: "Out NOW!"

I made a sweeping movement with my arm, pointing to the outside. And that was that! She was free! Halleluiah! We cried and danced around like school children. To see a loved one go from a tortured look to an angelic face is truly heavenly. These dear friends are fervent followers of Christ today and we thank God for them.

8

BLESSED BUG INVASION

O ur townhouse lease was up in Downsview. The search was on for a place close enough to the bakery in Aurora, to make travel up and down not so time consuming. With much prayer and searching the ads in newspapers we found a beautiful house in Keswick. It was situated on a hill just south of that little village. The owners could give us a two-year stay only, without a lease, but we trusted God for the future.

*   *

It was a dream moving into this house in October 1974. Windows from floor to ceiling were on both levels to be able to have an unobstructed view of the lake. As we looked out of our wall-to-wall windows, we enjoyed quite a sight of cottages and streets leading to the edge of Cook's Bay, which was the most southern part of Lake Simcoe. We had 4 bedrooms upstairs and downstairs there were two, big enough to rent it out to someone who needed a place also. The backyard was not big and did not have a slope but a straight down drop of about 35 feet. No fence to protect our children from falling if they were to lose their footing. That was the only drawback; we just had to warn them continuously to stay away from the edge. It was not a rocky wall, but sandy soil. There was a bit of a slope on the bottom of that hill from erosion, which made it not as dangerous if one were to slide down by accident. Well, the older ones thought it was great fun to just slide down if they wanted to visit the neighbors in the cottages below us.

* *

Zach went to grade 1 in September that year. I would get the little ones dressed and ready early in the morning to walk him to the school bus, which picked up a couple of children at the corner of Beverley Drive and the Queensway. After a couple of weeks two neighbor girls offered to pick Zach up from the house and walk him to the bus, and in the afternoon walk him home. That was a blessing! I could take a bit longer to ease into the day. After the little ones were fed and dressed, I could relax with a cup of coffee. Some days a sister-in-the-Lord would join me in the morning and study the scriptures. If we had a question, we would search out the answer. She had a little girl who would play with Arjan as they were about the same age. Stephanie and Joshua were little buddies and played in the middle of the living room, as her and I had a bit of fellowship.

* *

The next year was a "mosquito" year. These pesky insects were around our neighborhood in large numbers! When the girls came to pick up Zach to go to the bus, I saw a cloud of them surround the threesome. Their tiny wings would reflect the sunlight like little diamonds. Even though they were mosquitoes and nasty to have around, it still was a beautiful sight. I felt sorry for the children as they were swinging their arms around trying to keep them from landing on parts of their bodies not covered by clothing. Michael had set up a big tent in the backyard, so the children could play outside without getting bothered too much. I would spray the outside edge of the door with some bug-spray to minimize the number of insects entering the play area. Michael suggested that we walk around the parameter of our lot, pray and anoint the 4 corners with oil. That was an excellent idea, and we agreed to do it as soon as the children were in bed. After our prayers, my husband and I felt satisfied that something good was going to happen. We had no idea how or what but gave the outcome in the Hands of the Lord.

*   *

One beautiful sunny morning, about 14 days after our prayers, I was sitting at the dining room table in front of the sliding door. The door was open, screen door closed, and I was facing the window, reading some scriptures. As I looked outside, I saw something flying by the house. Not just one, but many flying insects! The children and I walked out on the deck to see what they were. Some were caught in the tent and we went down to the backyard to see if we could see one close-up. Dragonflies!

They were flying in droves from south to north, like an endless procession. As this was going on for some time, I wondered whether this was a normal occurrence. The children and I were standing together in the yard with these dragonflies all around us. Then I remembered I had an Audubon Nature Encyclopedia, ran inside and took the book that contained the information on dragonflies. Another name was given after dragonflies: Mosquito hawks! Once back outside I relayed the news to the children: their nickname is mosquito hawk as they eat mosquitoes while flying. We were thanking the Lord for sending insects that feast on these unpopular insects. I wanted to know if it was normal for dragonflies to fly in such large numbers from south to north. It did not specify any kind of information in the encyclopedia, so I phoned the Department of Natural Recourses in Ontario. Their location was in Maple at that time. The gentleman on the other end was not sure what I was asking and connected me to the professor who was available to answer my questions. After telling him about the hordes of dragonflies over our house and neighborhood for the last 10 minutes, he said:

"I have never heard of this before."

I encouraged him to come quickly to see for himself. He laughed and said:

"You really think they will still be there? It will take me at least an hour to come to Keswick."

In my excitement I had not considered the distance between Maple and Keswick. By the time I was finished with the telephone call, the dragonflies had already diminished in numbers. And so were the mosquitoes! I did not really notice it until the next morning when Zach and the two neighbor girls were making their way to the school bus. What a difference! Sure, there were still some these 'bitey' things flying around, but not in abundance anymore!

When something like that takes place in nature, as an answer to prayer, you know that it is God's Hand that provides the relief. What a testimony to His grace towards His children in need.

*   *

As we did not have the technology in that year to search the internet, I did so once we had a computer. I found a web site that mentioned dragonflies in large amounts hovering over a lake in the northern part of the US. They called it a 'mysterious phenomenon' even though they were stationary over that lake, not moving together from one area to another.

As I am writing this in the age of technology, and we can research anything and everything on the internet, I have found more accounts of a couple of people witnessing swarms of dragonflies flying in a distinctive pattern mostly over landmarks such as ridges and shorelines. It is still called a 'phenomenon'! With the research that is going on, there are yet many questions about the behaviour of these swarming gifts of nature.

I just thank God for such marvels of creation.

9

TONSILITIS

Many trips were made to the family physician when Zach and Arjan were 7 and 5 years old. We had these boys on antibiotics just about every 3 months. The culprit was their tonsils. On the last visit to the doctor, he told me that if their condition had not improved in the spring of the next year, he would schedule them for a tonsillectomy.

* *

It was in the start of the new year that Arjan had a very sore throat. Not until after he had gone to bed that the fever started. I always checked our children before going to bed and noticed that his head was warmer but not burning up. I planned to give him some medicine to control the fever in the morning.

My husband was getting ready to go to work at 6 am and my little guy had woken up and had made his way to the bathroom. I was woken up by the sound of Arjan being sick to his stomach. In an instant I was at the bathroom door. Disturbed by the look of his body in distress I tried to calm him. His little legs were stomping on the floor as he was choking on food particles. His tonsils must have been so swollen that it had narrowed his throat. In a panic I yelled at my husband as he was going out of the door:

"Michael come here, quick!"

He made his way back into the house to where he heard my call. There we stood looking at my son, my tears flowing and feeling very helpless.

"Please pray for him before you go" I begged.

My husband laid his hand on his hot head and made a simple request to God for healing. After a minute or so, Arjan stopped vomiting and was able to breathe again without a problem. My anxious feelings began to subside. Then Michael kissed his little boy and went to work. For about 10 minutes I sat on the side of his bed to make sure he was asleep before I made my way to my own bed, with the doors open so I could hear him if he would wake up again. No more repeats of the struggle he experienced early that morning and there was peace until the household was buzzing with preparations for school. Even with the noises of children having breakfast and playing, Arjan did not wake up.

We had our 2 oldest children enrolled in the Holland Marsh Christian School. It was time for me to drive Zach to school. I went downstairs to the living quarters of my sister-in-law Ria, who came to live with us after our renters moved into a little house of their own. I asked her if she did not mind keeping the door open to the upstairs to listen for any signs or sounds of a waking boy. Arjan was still sound asleep as I took Zach and the 2 younger children for a ride from Keswick to the Holland Marsh. The trip there and back took about an hour, so I expected Arjan to be awake when I came home. But it was so quiet in the house that I immediately tiptoed to his bedroom and found him still sound asleep. I was thankful that after such a traumatic event in his young life, he was getting a good rest.

* *

After notifying Ria that I was home, I started emptying the dishwasher. Most likely the clanging of the dishes woke Arjan up and he came running towards me:

"Mommy, Mommy, I'm all better!"

What a beautiful sound to hear him so clear and running to me, like a normal energetic little boy should. We never went back to the doctor for tonsillitis, not for Arjan or Zach. We were in awe and to be truthful, I was waiting for it to happen again. God had to do some work in me to trust that His healing is permanent.

* *

Not until many years later that I realized that the healing touch of Jesus was not just the two older boys, but on each of the children that were born after them. At this writing all of our 10 children still have their tonsils.

10

CAMPING 1975

One of the joys of a Canadian summer for our family was camping halfway through August in one of the Provincial Parks in Ontario. We choose that time as there were fewer blackflies or mosquitoes than early in the season, as the heat and dry periods in the previous months would kill most of them.

Driving up to Grundy Provincial Park over Hwy 11 and take the ferry over Georgian Bay from Manitoulin Island back was our plan. For our family to go on such a big ferry boat was quite an experience! In the years to come we have sailed across Huron Bay quite a few times enjoying the wind and the waves in calm weather.

When the wind was strong, and the whitecaps would be on the water I would go sit outside in the front of the boat to watch the ferry cutting through the choppy lake as I became quite nauseous without the fresh air. Still, I did not want to miss out being on the water and see the joy on the faces of our children.

* *

At that time our youngest child Joshua was almost a year and a half. Stephanie would turn 3 in September and the two oldest boys were 6 and 5 years old. Setting up the tent and putting a tarp over the area overhead to endure any wet days in comfort took some planning and time, but my husband proved to be very ingenious in this area. Right in front of the tent door he set up another tarp to keep the sand and dirt to a minimum inside our temporary abode. We hiked a lot and Joshua would sit in a little carrier that Michael would have on his back. The child would sit quite high and could look over Dad's head which was great if Emil would judge the height properly going through the bush, so Joshua did not end up with his little face in the overhanging branches.

For her young age Stephanie was quite a little trooper walking alongside of her 2 older brothers. As our walks would never be short, she needed a lift on our way back to the tent and I would take her on my hip and had no problem carrying her for 3 miles as she would cling to me like a little monkey would to cling to the fur of its mother. She grabbed my top, and her little legs would be snug around my body. I loved every minute of our walks.

*   *

Around supper time we made a fire for the children to roast some marshmallows for dessert and we would sing children songs, some of which would be songs to and about Jesus. Our neighbors had quite a few children and they played very well with our older boys. We became friends during the time that we camped in Grundy. At night when the children would be in bed, we sat around the dying embers of the fire and shared family stories as well as the good news of the gospel.

*   *

They were devout Catholics, and it was easy to guide them into a relationship with Jesus Christ. I shared how even though we had 4 children, we had a desire to have one more girl. To get pregnant had been no problem up to that time and had expected to be with child as soon as I would stop nursing the previous baby. That was not the case this time around.

We shared our hopes for the future with our newfound friends, so I told them about the word that the Lord had given me one night after that we had discussed the desire to have another daughter. I was not doubting that it would come to pass. We just had to wait. I promised to let her know as soon as I was with child. Quite a few questions were answered and encouraging words accepted before the time came for us and our friends to return home. We exchanged some personal information and made sure we had each other's telephone number. What joy we felt on our way back home.

* *

Once we were back into the daily routine of child rearing and Michael working in the business of baking healthy bread, we shared the conversion of our camping neighbors to close friends, when they asked if we had been in contact with them, I told them that we felt to give them some time before we would give them a call.

* *

Halfway October I knew I was expecting our fifth child and called our camping buddies. What a surprise to hear their excitement at the other end of the line. They were totally committed to follow Christ.

In their community was a small Catholic church which was transformed by their zeal and even the statues of the saints were taken out of there. That was certainly not something one would do singlehanded. There must have been quite some people that were transformed by their message of salvation in order to see such a change in a church.

Connection has been lost since then, and we hoped and prayed that even when tested and tried these followers of Christ would not lose their excitement of their 'first love' and continue in the faith.

11

ACCIDENTAL ANOMALY

Late spring 1976. It was close to the end of the school year and we were looking forward to the summer. It was to be a nice break from driving Zach and Arjan to and from school in the Holland Marsh for a couple of months. We had 4 children at that time, Stephanie our only girl was 3. I was about 7 ½ months into my fifth pregnancy. The Christian elementary school was half an hour drive from our home in Keswick. Every morning I packed the children and their school bags in the 1972 Chrysler New Yorker and made the trip with the 4 children to arrive there at 9 am. Picking up time was 3:30 pm.

Unthinkable for these days, but there were no baby seats and no seatbelts at that time, so a Mom did what she thought was the safest way to transport children in a car. Joshua who had turned 2 in March was placed close to me on the front seat and any time I put my foot on the brake, my right arm went instinctively in front of the little man to stop him from sliding forward.

Zach, Arjan and Stephanie were to sit ON the backseat. There was a constant word going to the back, for them to stay down. Often, I glanced in my rear-view mirror and I sometimes would see them like sailors in a boat standing on the seat going left when I turned left and leaning right while turning right.

"Sit down guys!" would be my command.

It took some stern words at times or a threat to stop the car before they obeyed.

* *

On a beautiful sunny day, I was on my way back home from the Marsh Christian School. There were no stoplights at that time on Bathurst street and Hwy 11. It was not a busy crossing, but always one had to wait patiently at the stop sign, and I and took no chances with my precious cargo. A Volkswagen was coming from the north to the left of our position and a pickup truck was across from us at the other side of Hwy 11. I saw that the driver across from us was unaware of the approaching car on the highway. He was not waiting, I started shouting at the pickup truck driver as if he could hear me. In my mind, it was like slow motion as the Volkswagen hit the back of the pickup as he was coming towards me.

As I was yelling: "Nooo!!" the children made their way to their feet to see what I was so upset about. The Volkswagen slammed into the right side of the pickup truck, with the truck now swinging its back side around. The force of speed made it spin a 180 degree turn and hit our front on the left, just denting the radiator and taking out the left corner and buckling the hood. On impact Stephanie was thrown from the backseat to the front as I hung onto little Joshua with my right arm and bracing myself with my left arm straight out clasping the steering wheel with white knuckles, hoping it would keep my pregnant belly safe from a hit. All the children cried and shrieked at the same time and it was mayhem to say the least. As soon as the initial shock of the crash was over, I wanted to gather all the children in my arms to calm them and give them a sense of safety.

I tried to open my door, but it was jammed, could not scoot over to the right as my belly was being squeezed into the steering wheel. I was quite calm up to that point but feeling trapped and not able to hug my children, I lost my cool, wept and cried out loud to God.

* *

In a panic, one does not think things through, as later I just put the steering wheel in a higher position and scooted out on the right side. That right door opened without any problem as a lady came in and sat on the front seat. She did not introduce herself, or asked how we were doing, but took Stephanie on her lap. She was calming that little girl and her soothing words had a tranquil effect on all of us. After that the peace returned, she stepped out of the car with a greeting and a most beautiful smile. At that moment sensibility returned to my mind and figured a way out of my seat. We made our way outside where I had a chance to hold my children close, thanking God that we were all safe. After the hugs and the drying of the tears, people from the other cars gathered around us making sure that nobody was injured. Aside from some bruises, all looked good. I asked where the lady was that helped us, so I could thank her. The occupants of the other cars pointed to the woman that was in a car behind us.

"No, she was much younger and had long hair" I replied.

"Sorry Ma'am but that is the only woman here".

I looked around again in the hope that they were wrong, so I could show her my gratitude. Surprised that she was nowhere to be seen, I kept the mystery in my heart and thanked Jesus for the wonderful peace that came to us through that lady's care, during such a disturbing event.

* *

The driver of the Volkswagen was badly shaken but could walk around. After that I exchanged insurance information with the pickup truck owner and myself. The truck had quite a bit of damage to the back only. The driver of the pick-up showed no injury to his body but was very confused.

The police had arrived quite soon after the accident. He investigated and interviewed the occupants of the cars present at the moment of impact. Then he ordered the cars behind us to back up so we could all get out of the tight squeeze that we found ourselves in, as the first two cars were pushed into the third vehicle. A gentleman from one of the cars checked out our New Yorker told me I could drive even though there was front end damage. I packed my kids in the back seat with a stern word to stay seated.

Thankfully, our car had a long front end that even the damage to the whole left corner had not touched the parts necessary for driving. Later that night as I was telling the story to my husband it became clear that the Lord had sent a longhaired angel to comfort and be a calm in the midst of a storm.

Are they not all ministering spirits sent forth for those who will inherit salvation? Heb. 1:14

12

JERUSHA

In 1974 we were blessed with 3 boys and 1 girl. The desire to have 4 children was fulfilled and our family was complete.

When Joshua was 9 months old, my husband said that he would really like to have another girl. I so enjoyed my babies that I immediately agreed. I nursed my children until they were 1 year old and knew would not fall pregnant until the last baby was weaned. That was just the way the Lord had made me. We did not close off the possibility for another child after Joshua was a year old. The clothes that were not worn anymore by the last baby were cleaned and put away in a closet, not given away.

Michael was busy in the Health food bakery that we owned and operated, and I was able stay home after Stephanie was born. Since production days were 36 hours long from Sunday till mid-Monday and Wednesday till mid-Thursday, there were days I did not see my husband, unless I would go and visit him if I had my mother-in-law to look after the children.

* *

One of these evenings that I was alone at home I watched a movie called Hawaii. One plot summary was written by Jim Beaver:

- Abner Hale, a rigid and humorless New England missionary, marries the beautiful Jerusha Bromley and takes her to the exotic island kingdom of Hawaii, intent on converting the natives. But the clash between the two cultures is too great and instead of understanding there comes tragedy.

When watching this movie, it became clear that this missionary Abner Hale was strict and emotionally cold while his wife Jerusha was a picture of grace, warmth and strength.

Close to the end of the movie the Lord spoke to me and said that we shall have a girl and her name will be Jerusha. I felt such a joy and excitement and looked forward to the time to see the fulfillment of that promise. Joshua was one year old in March and nothing happened; no pregnancy after I weaned my boy. Because of the promise it was not hard to wait, but thinking of Abraham and Sarah, I prayed it would not take 25 years.

After our camping holiday I noticed a change in my body and knew we were going to have our daughter in June the next year. We had moved to Keswick, where we were able to rent that beautiful home with many bedrooms, one small one just for the new baby.

* *

We expected Jerusha on June 24, 1976 and all was ready at that time to welcome her. I went for my check-ups to a doctor in Aurora and thus was slated to have the birth at the

Newmarket hospital. All was well, except for the due date. I was always a little later than the date that was figured out by the doctor. I was not in any rush, but since we had an early and very hot summer, I did not mind having her earlier than later. By the 2nd of July, my contractions started in the late afternoon. The female doctor suggested that I make my way to the hospital as it was my 5th and did not want to take a chance for me to have that baby on my way there. Labor was progressing nicely and having Michael by my side was a real comfort. The rules for fathers to be at the birth of their children had just changed 2 years before, and they were allowed be in the room. Since I had to get everything in order at home to be absent for a couple of days, I was tired and thankful to be in a bed. I relished the thought of having my little daughter in my arms within the next couple of hours. The nurses asked me what I hoped for and I told them that it was a girl. "How do you know" that was their question, and I related to them the promise I received a year and a half earlier. No ultrasounds were in use at that time as that did not become a common practice until the 1990's.

*   *

Once the night set in I fell asleep, and the contractions stopped all together. After I woke up and noticed that I was without pain, I was a bit concerned and asked the nurses if I should just go home and not take up a bed that someone else might have need of. They contacted the Dr Betty K. and she said for me not to worry but to stay where I was. Michael stayed also and tried to get comfortable in a hard chair. That morning Dr. Betty examined me and since I was only 3 cm dilated, she first wanted an X-ray to make sure I was not having twins. After that she would start an Oxytocin drip around noon. The X-ray confirmed that I was carrying only one baby, of which I had no doubt even before the test. I never had any medication to speed up labor before and this was not something I was looking forward to. Labor started up again before noon after some walking around and I hoped that the drip was not going to be administered. The doctor thought it better to get labor going a bit stronger and as she had said earlier, since it was my 5th baby it would not take long before she would be entering the world.

* *

With Michael on my right side and the doc on my left in her street clothes they started the drip. I had a monitor on my belly to check the baby's heart rate, which compared to today's instruments, was huge and quite uncomfortable. I asked Dr. Betty how long she was planning the drip. By this time it was 5:30 pm and she said that she would allow it till 11:30 at night and then leave me to do it on my own. She checked me frequently and was surprised I was still only 3 cm. I thought with all that pain and hardly any breaks between contractions I was ready to deliver that baby. It came to a point that I was in so much pain that I was shaking my head back and forth. Michael got up and called the pastor of the little community church in Keswick that we were attending at that time. He relayed the situation that even though I had labored already for so many hours in great pain and still was not ready to push.

* *

Pastor Mike called some older ladies, prayer warriors, and they agreed together that this baby was going to be born at 9 pm that evening. This was not known to anyone but the women.

Around 8:55 pm I could not handle the pain anymore. My lower back was in flames and I was crying and shaking my head saying:

"No more, I can't do this anymore!"

Dr. Betty checked me once more and told me that I was not anymore dilated than 4 cm. If I did not have the promise for this baby I would have screamed and told her to take that needle out of my arm. Then a thought came and asked if I could be on my side, thinking it might relieve the pressure of my back.

"Of course, you can".

Because of that big monitor on my belly, the 2 nurses that were in the room with me, carefully held it in place while I turned on my side. They had to readjust it a bit to make sure they heard the baby's heartbeat. As soon as I was off my back, the searing pain became bearable, and I said:

"The baby is coming!"

"It can't be" was Dr. Betty's response and checked.

Jerusha's head was crowning, and the doc ran out of the door to get changed into her greens. It was 9:05 pm and the nurses were the ones that helped our daughter make quite an entrance into this world. Dr. Betty returned and did the rest of the routine after the birth.

"I cannot believe it" she said, "I'm sorry I was not there for her birth".

I gladly excused her as I was in a bit of heaven at that time. Thanking and praising God that our promise was in my arms.

* *

After a little while, Michael phoned the family and Pastor Mike. Not until the Sunday service the next day, that Michael found out what the ladies had agreed on, that the baby was to be born at 9:00 pm. It must have been quite a boost of faith for them. As for Michael and me, we were amazed at the goodness of God; that His promises are yes and amen.

13

"LOAVES" AND FISHES

Around the time that Jerusha was expected, Michael experienced a God moment of his own, and will tell his story here:

We had 2 days of baking in a week, to supply the Health Food stores in Toronto and surrounding areas with fresh baked goods. Wednesday was one of those days. We started at 6 am and were not done baking and packing till Thursday afternoon. Most of the time we worked a 36-hour workday. As we had a couple that did most of the deliveries in the city, I still had a few clients to supply with what they had ordered around Aurora. That was my job for Friday. I also had to pick up ingredients for the next bake. As I was doing the deliveries, my mind was not on my driving, but on what all was to be done yet before the weekend. As a result, I was driving too fast and got pulled over by the police. He did not just give me a ticket for going over the speed limit but took me to the station for unpaid speeding tickets. There I was, locked up and I did not even have enough money to pay the outstanding fines.

* *

I used to work in Newmarket before I started the Health Food business and the police station where I was held, was in that town. I phoned my old boss and hoped he was able to bail me out. He was very gracious and paid my fines. By the time I was back in my car it was too late to get the ingredients I needed for the bake on Sunday, which were to be picked up in Toronto. Only one supplier of bakery ingredients was carrying the special flour I used for our bread and other health-food baked goods, such as cinnamon Danishes, muffins and cookies, to name a few. It was stone-ground, whole-wheat flour, and it was sold only by a flour mill in Toronto. Normally I would need 6 bags of flour.

* *

When I came in the bakery that Sunday morning, I had 1 bag and a bit in another one. It hit me hard that there was not enough to fill the orders. What to do? I was born-again but my walk and relationship with Jesus was not as it should have been. My prayer to God was:

"Lord you have to help me here, make the flour last until I'm done baking".

I started to scoop and mix and mix and scoop! By the end of the bake, I still had half a bag left!

Jesus was so gracious and met me in my need and time of trouble. Years later taking inventory of my life, I realized what a big miracle had taken place.

Grace: unmerited favour!

We do not deserve God's grace and favour, but He also sees the end from the beginning. Even when saved and washed in His Blood, He allows us to go through testing and trial, to make us stronger in faith as we continue in love towards God first and our fellow man second.

PART 2

PART 2

14

"THE MOVE" SAM FIFE CULT

You foolish Galatians! Who has bewitched you? Before your very eyes Jesus Christ was clearly portrayed as crucified. ² I would like to learn just one thing from you: Did you receive the Spirit by the works of the law, or by believing what you heard? ³ Are you so foolish? After beginning by means of the Spirit, are you now trying to finish by means of the flesh? Galatians 3:1-3

Some ministries have the stamp of approval of Christ upon their work of faith and see a great outpouring of the Holy Spirit, yet do not continue in the truth. In search of why this sometimes happens to fellowships, a pastor or a spiritual leader after a revival or an awakening, sent me on an investigative trip through many websites.

As the fellowship that we attended in the 1976 was an outflow of Sam Fife Ministry, I was interested in how this man became such an influence in the lives of so many believers. The information about this man is on Google. Sam Fife became a Baptist minister in 1957 and received the 'Baptism in the Holy Spirit" while he was pastoring a church in New Orleans. In one of the prayer meetings, he attended in 1963, he felt he had received a divine revelation of God. He preached this revelation all over the States, starting new groups or assemblies. They called themselves "The Move of God" and after some time it became known by "The Move" not to have any association with other Christian groups or denominations or their doctrine. He believed the revelation he received and preached was that the time was near for only a selected group of followers to reach "a state of sinless perfection", and through them God would manifest Himself to the world. But first they needed to go through some special dealings that God Himself would orchestrate.

Fife was a staunch believer in and taught the doctrine that the normal aging process had stopped for him and thus he was 'immortal'. He would not give a straight answer to questions about his age, he would just say: "I AM".

Sam Fife died in 1979 while flying his private plane with 3 of his followers through heavy fog, crashing into a mountainside in Guatemala. He was only 54 years old.

* *

When pastors exalt themselves to a certain platform and preach that the Lord elevated them to that state, it is in fact their own pride and greed that are the deceiving factors, and one can expect the Hand of God to come down hard on them.

For the pastors are become brutish, and have not sought the Lord; therefore they shall not prosper, and all their flocks shall be scattered. Jeremiah 10:21 KJV

* *

Why this man's theology was so attractive in the 70s is easy to understand, as it was a time of social unrest, with many young people searching for inspiration. Among his followers he was considered an apostle. He had a certain vision of the end-times, and many bought into his interpretation of certain scriptures passages dealing with what was to come. A group of ministers believed in this end-time message and underscored it in submitting to Fife and his 'Wilderness Message' which he started to preach in 1971. The 'Wilderness message' as Fife understood and propagated it was based on Matthew 24:7-22:

Nation will rise against nation, and kingdom against kingdom. There will be famines and earthquakes in various places. 8 All these are the beginning of birth pains.9 "Then you will be handed over to be persecuted and put to death, and you will be hated by all nations because of me. 10 At that time many will turn away from the faith and will betray and hate each other, 11 and many false prophets will appear and deceive many people. 12 Because of the increase of wickedness, the love of most will grow cold, 13 but the one who stands firm to the end will be saved. 14 And this gospel of the kingdom will be preached in the whole world as a testimony to all nations, and then the end will come.

15 "So when you see standing in the holy place 'the abomination that causes desolation,'[a] spoken of through the prophet Daniel—let the reader understand—16then let those who are in Judea flee to the mountains.17Let no one on the housetop go down to take anything out of the house.18Let no one in the field go back to get their cloak.19How dreadful it will be in those days for pregnant women and nursing mothers!20Pray that your flight will not take place in winter or on the Sabbath.21For then there will be great distress, unequaled from the beginning of the world until now—and never to be equaled again.

22 "If those days had not been cut short, no one would

survive, but for the sake of the elect those days will be shortened.

Also, Revelation 12:6 was taken literally:

⁶ The woman fled into the wilderness to a place prepared for her by God, where she might be taken care of for 1,260 days.

In the next couple of years communal farms sprang up in Alaska, the BC mountains in Canada and Columbia. Thousands of believers sold their homes, moved there and combined their resources to truly have everything in common. They were little self-containing villages. They did not need to rely on anything or anyone from the outside world, as the ones that were gifted in certain areas, shared their abilities. This may sound comforting as the participants felt a real sense of family and safety. Yet members were to totally submit to the rules of the local ministry and the reality is that humanity in their sinful state fall prey to pride when in a position of such authority. Leaders became rulers or little dictators. In later years, stories of abuse surfaced as members found their way back into society. Physical, psychological and sexual abuse was reported, but spiritual damage was sustained by demanding complete submission to the leaders.

This man Fife must have had some amazing charisma, to have such a large number of believers turn their back on sound doctrine.

This information was not in my possession until after we left the little fellowship and quite some years later, when the Google websites were available. Our leader had a certain charisma too, and persuasive powers to keep *'a flock that wanted to please the Lord in all things'* following what he preached. In the later years his ways were opposite of the Gospel of Christ.

15

'THE FELLOSHIP' A CHRISTIAN CULT

The man that was the leader over a small group of believers was in this 'Move' and did not believe that he and his family were to relocate to one of those farms. This group came together every Sunday and held their own services. When we first attended these 'get-togethers' we did not see any difference in their belief than of any other Full Gospel Evangelistic Church.

We were introduced to this group through Mother and Father M.

A BBQ was organized, and we were invited with our children to *Opa* and *Oma's* house.

It was wonderful and enjoyed the night with song and stories. We felt quite comfortable, and since at that time we did not attend a church that believed or practised the Pentecostal experience we agreed to join. Also, the family connection helped make the transition easy. The scripture in Mark 12:30-31 was truly in practise.

30 Love the Lord your God with all your heart and with all your soul and with all your mind and with all your strength. [a]

31 The second is this: 'Love your neighbor as yourself.'[b] There is no commandment greater than these."

Services often lasted 3 hours and we were encouraged to follow 1 Cor 14:26

What then shall we say, brothers and sisters? When you come together, each of you has a hymn, or a word of instruction, a revelation, a tongue or an interpretation. Everything must be done so that the church may be built up.

Many Sundays we had a meal together, had great fellowship and looked after each other's children. We felt loved and taken care of. The worship was truly heavenly with harmonizing voices and just one instrument, a guitar played by a sister-in-the-Lord. There was nothing fancy, but each of the members had a heart to glorify God. We experienced the sweet presence of the Lord in these meetings.

The Lord inhabits the praises of His people. Psalm 22:3 KJV

It was in this atmosphere that certain scriptures were used to sway the members into accepting some of the ways of "The Move". The change was so gradual that we were like "the frog in tepid water, brought to a boil slowly". We would have been totally against any of these dogmas, had they come on a checklist in the beginning of our joining this fellowship. The persuasions were enforced by dreams, visions and 'prophecies' I have always believed that the Lord gives dreams and visions. Sometimes He will point to something in my own heart as a guide when I asked for a solution to a situation in my own life. The dreams and visions that many members of this fellowship had, were used to correct and guide others, not just oneself. As this was the acceptable way of interpretation, it is amazing how fast one will adapt to this lifestyle. The enemy of our souls will use anything to avert the attention of our own sinfulness and point to others. If one did not submit to correction given through a dream by someone else, you were considered rebellious. Since the scripture tells us that "rebellion is as the sin of witchcraft" one would submit and accept whatever interpretation was given by the dreamer or the leader.

They worship me in vain; their teachings are merely human rules. Matthew 15:9

The first big commandment was that we could not go to doctors or dentists anymore. That was extremely hard for me as I have always had worked in health care, either as a student in nursing in Holland and a lab technician in Canada. Using my knowledge in times of need in my family was a benefit rather than a hindrance. I realized that I was considered rebellious in this area and often cried out to God for more faith to believe Him for everything. As time passed it became easier to submit quickly and feel peace to obey to what was laid out before me. To please the Lord and to do what is right had been very important to me since I committed my life to Him, but in that kind of environment one starts to transfer the submission we are to have to the Lord, to the leaders. Scriptures were taken out of context and twisted to suit their ideas of how we were to believe and live. Faith in the Lord was mixed with fear of reprisals; that became a familiarity. Although I never lost my closeness with Jesus, I was so aware of the eyes of man on just about every move I made.

* *

I was to forget everything I had learned in nursing, but when one had an accident, needed stitches or wound care; I was relied upon to look after it. We accepted the dress code: Long skirts, long sleeves and for the men long pants even for the young children. No scissor was ever to touch a woman's hair and the men were to have it short. That was not hard for me but the pressure of these rules on our children in the ensuing years was a very sore spot in my heart, and theirs.

* *

The health food bakery business that my husband operated became a place of employment for several members. He was a patient man and taught some of them how to bake bread and other items that we sold to the health food stores in the Greater Toronto Area. In the winter months the orders for the health food stores were not as big, and Michael started to include white bread and buns and pastries to keep the business afloat. He was a pastry baker trained in the Netherlands, so he had the expertise to succeed in this area. It was needful to make enough money to pay the employees as some members had large families also. That was a tough act to follow even in the early 1980's through a deep recession.

* *

Christmas and Easter were not celebrated anymore as they had their origin in paganism. Even on birthdays there were to be no parties, but within the safety of our home we acknowledged that our children were gifted by God to us on that special day. Proper words and names were to be used, and no joking was allowed. Even the ones that were quite benign like a word play or a funny story, they were to be cut out of our lives. Yet we were never too hard on each other if we got together with other members, which most likely made life bearable. One such story was told to me by a sister, and we had a good laugh. She had gone to a butcher shop with her children and used the word 'children' a couple of times to address them. The storekeeper was impressed and gave her a compliment, she then explained that kids were baby goats and therefore not to be used for the children. On exiting the store, the children lingered a bit and she said in a loud voice: "Come on kids!" at which time the butcher must have raised an eyebrow or two. There were no reprisals as there was no dream or talk to others about her transgression.

* *

The cohesion between most of the followers in this group was great. We genuinely loved each other and taught one another the art of sewing, canning and childcare. The freedom of choosing for our children to have an education beyond 16 years of age was taken away. That was another rebellious time for my husband and me, as the leader was now telling us how we were to direct our children for their future.

* *

Vacations were not needed anymore as we were not having any stress if we followed the rules. Surely the peace of God was constant and a rest for our bodies and a change of scenery was unnecessary according to the leaders. Our family planned in secret, and we did manage to go camping twice, in the first year with Mom and Dad M to Mikisew Provincial Park and a second time more at the end of our connection with 'the Fellowship'. That second time we set up our campsite in the dark and unbeknown to us, we pitched our tent in the middle of a patch of poison ivy. Of course, when we noticed we thought that we were going to be punished by God for going against the rules. Not one of us had a rash and had a wonderful family time and fully enjoying nature's bounty in trees, bushes and wildflowers. That experience underscored our feeling that it was not God that was against having a vacation, but that the head of the fellowship would maybe lose his grip on us.

* *

On occasion we had visitors from other cities of Canada and also from the United States. They had a previous connection with "the Move" but did not heed the call from Sam Fife to move to the farms. I am sure there must have been quite a few followers that had a change of heart, but still kept many of "The Move" beliefs alive.

Owning a camera, making and saving pictures was also against the rules. We had a camera and saved our pictures in the bottom of a closet. Many were sent to the Netherlands so my Mom and Dad could see the children in different stages of their life. On many occasions I would send a roll of film so my Mom would develop them and send pictures back to me. I kept quiet about that hiding place but did ask the Lord to reveal to me if it was wrong. I put out a fleece before Him and petitioned that if a visitor from the States would have a prophecy and tell me that I had a secret in the closet, I would get rid of them. I still have all the pictures!!

* *

We got THE surprise of our 'Fellowship' time when our bed broke and we bought a cheap bedroom set. An open rebuke about the money we spend on ourselves was delivered on the next Sunday meeting. Nothing was to be purchased without the approval of the leaders. Why did we stay as long as we did? Fear that if we would step outside of the fellowship we would surely go to hell. The Lord would not look upon us with favour anymore.

* *

Michael had a great burden, that if we were to step out, we would have to close the bakery. He had a large family to support. There would be quite a few without a job, some of them also with large families. In the recession of the early 80's, the bakery business declined; Michael was suggested that he declare bankruptcy so that a couple of members who had enough money could start another bakery in Bradford. He did declare bankruptcy and was asked to manage the new bakery. Even though he was not too keen on doing that and after taking time to check out other bakeries to work in without success, he accepted the position and worked in that bakery for several years.

Once the leader moved north to start another fellowship, we felt free to talk amongst each other and learned quickly how the other members felt about most of the rules and regulations. We disbanded but it took almost a year for me to read the Word solely according to the Holy Spirit interpretation and not according to the leader of that fellowship. On many occasions we felt that we had lost 11 years of our lives but speaking out forgiveness to those that had put us into bondage helped us over that resentment. When the feeling of anger rose up about the treatment we received, we forgave again and again. It is the best way to find healing for hurting hearts.

* *

After some time, we joined the Vineyard in Barrie and found freedom and warm fellowship with the family of God, reconnecting with some families that had left a couple of years before. Still in all the years that we were under this kind of oppression, nothing that we went through either by our own choice or circumstance, is lost to the Lord!

And we know that in all things God works for the good of those who love him, who have been called according to his purpose. Romans 8:28

Certainly, we did not grow as we could have in our walk with the Lord in those years, but I know that He was my close companion through all the struggles that I went through. I prayed in tongues a lot and sought Him in tears when feeling overwhelmed. He blessed our family with health, answered my prayers and worked miracles in spite of where we fellowshipped.

16

NEWMARKET

The move from Keswick to Newmarket was in the summer of 1977.

From a beautiful stately home overlooking the most southern point of Lake Simcoe, to an old farmhouse was a huge adjustment for the whole family. We were encouraged to have Michael's Mom and Dad move in with us, as their lease had come to an end in Richmond Hill. I loved my in-laws and never had an issue with them and did not think about it very long. We signed a lease for 2 years. Those years proved to be very trying and challenging as the fellowship that we committed ourselves to, became more controlling. The scripture and song that I kept in my heart was:

"I know in whom I have believed and am convinced that he is able to guard what I have entrusted to him until that day." 2 Timothy 1:12

I committed myself, my husband and my children to the Lord and deep down within my heart I knew He was our keeper and would work things out even though we struggled in following the "rules" of the fellowship. Today I find comfort in the knowledge that in the Lord an experience is never lost. He will use it to make you wiser in the choices you make in your future. Making you more sensitive to certain teachings that are in Christian circles that could lead you astray once more.

*   *

There was a huge barn behind the house on a good piece of property.

Surrounded by huge fields with grass at least knee high, the area behind the house looked like it belonged in a place that had maybe 30-40 inhabitants, but on the south, there was Newmarket, on the west Hwy 11 and across from us was the house of a doctor, a veterinarian, who became famous because of his brand of dog food. A commercial was made for this dog food at his property and a helicopter was used to film the action. Our children were hanging out of the bedroom window facing this house. It must have been the highlight of that year to them.

To the north we had a couple of houses along the highway. The neighbours right beside us proved to be wonderful people.

I missed the clean, spacious house that was our home for 2 years previously, with so much closet space that everything had a place that I never had to search for an item. But old farmhouses had no closets, no wardrobes and very few kitchen cupboards. One bedroom was set aside for Mom and Dad M, the two other bedrooms we divided over our 3 boys and 2 girls.

Above the kitchen was a large room that Michael and I changed into a bedroom.

We moved a lot of our belongings behind curtains that I

had hanging down from the lowest rafters. There were no ceilings or walls covered with drywall, it was all raw wood in that attic. It was quite rustic to say the least.

The children loved the big barn full of hay. There was swing in there and they would jump off at the highest point of the upswing and end up in the soft hay. Underneath that floor, there were a couple of pens that needed a bit of cleaning but were looking strong and safe for some livestock. It made it truly look like a homestead barn.

We were given the opportunity two buy 2 piglets. They were reasonably priced and cute looking too. With a family like ours, there would be plenty of leftovers for slop for these piggies.

*   *

At this point, we had our planned family of 5 children, a health food bakery and a healthy dose of energy to keep things together. That it was going to go through a great transformation in a short time, was not anticipated. Since we had started to go to 'The Fellowship', the guidelines that we had set out for our family were not according to God's word but according to the leaders. The first thing we had to get changed was birth control! Since my husband and I had our desired number of children, we felt our family was complete.

"The Lord opens and closes the womb" was the word. Not realizing that was just part of a scripture, I submitted without searching the scriptures for myself in this area. I wanted to be a pleasure unto the Lord in every area of my life. A new baby I would accept with open arms. My husband had the weight of providing for his family as the mothers were not allowed to enter the workplace. He said that the Lord had given us 5 beautiful children and that was our desire before entering in this 'Fellowship'. I understood his reasoning, but he surrendered to this new rule too. Our close-knit family held it together through the first year. That included Michael's Mom and Dad. At least Mom and I could bounce some things off each. Things that really bothered us we discussed and would pray for clarification and acceptance. We had peace as long as the leaders were not visiting us. As soon as someone was coming into the driveway, we tightened up. We got used to this too and felt the anxious feeling just in the first couple of years.

Amazing what one can get used or conditioned to.

* *

In that first year my Mom in Holland asked if my youngest sister could come to Canada for a year. We opened our home and heart and we found her a space in the girls' bedroom. A cousin from Germany came for a 3 week visit and we placed a bed in the large living room that was hardly ever used. We mostly stayed in the kitchen, close to the cooking woodstove in fall and winter, and in summer we also gathered in the front room. Michael's brother John came to live with us later and we kept the bed in the living room for him. A busy, bustling place for sure. Mom, my sister Quirina and Michael's sister Ria helped in the bakery with packing and deliveries. My job was to keep the fire going and look after the household. Cooking, canning and laundry besides the cleaning kept me busy in a good way. I loved cooking and trying out new recipes. Some of which became favorites for our growing family.

* *

One of the persuasions that this group had was the spiritualizing of every little thing that one went through physically. If you wore glasses, there was something wrong with your vision in the spirit. If one hurt a leg, your walk in the Lord was questioned, and so on. Jesus said:

"Do not judge, or you too will be judged". Matthew 7:1

A truer translation is: "Do not condemn or sentence". We should make 'righteous judgements' to keep us from falling into sin and spiritual idolatry.

"For in the same way you judge others, you will be judged, and with the measure you use, it will be measured to you". Matthew 7:2

In the following years in this group we learned to judge each other in a wrong way. It unknowingly became a vicious circle. We judged and were judged. If one became sick or had an injury, one might not dare to bring it up for prayer as immediate judgment was given, if not in word certainly in thought. It perpetuated fear. Jesus came to set us free but looking back the leadership only put more shackles on our ankles. It was not until around 1982 that I started to loosen myself from that grip. I will discuss more about that later.

Yet in all that, we worshipped the Lord in song and praise. The love between some of the members was real and still rings true today when we are in the company of each other.

17

JEREMIAH

I got pregnant with our 6th baby in the spring of 1977 when Jerusha was 10 months old. Usually, I did not get pregnant until I stopped nursing after the baby was a year old, but this time was different. The pregnancy was without any complications other than more varicose veins in my legs. My baby was expected in January 1978. It was quite strange not to visit a doctor; I did not dare, even if I wanted to go. Of course, I struggled in my heart, but put my fears and concerns at the feet of Jesus and in time it became a way of life.

* *

The summer before this birth was a busy one. Since we had connection to the group that grew many vegetables themselves, we received garbage bags full of them: green and yellow beans, carrots and beets, pickling cucumbers, and leafy greens. In addition, we would get a couple of bushels of grapes and peaches as some families would go to the Niagara region and pick their own fruits. Most of this harvest would find their way in my enormous collection of canning jars. Many were given to me and quite a bit more had to be bought. Dill pickles were a favorite amongst the family members, but also jams and jellies were stored in the cool basement.

Time went by quickly and the winter became a time of preparation for the new baby. The bassinet that was used for the previous children was taken out of storage, baby clothes washed and folded neatly and stored in the dresser that also served as a change-table. As it was going to be a homebirth, arrangements had to be made for the younger children to be with other members for about a week. Mother M and Mrs. M from 'The Fellowship' were going to be the midwives. They did not have any training in this area but were counting on the Lord for wisdom in these circumstances.

* *

At this time, we had about 10 families attending the fellowship. One couple had their baby in the summer of 1977, there were complications and the baby died. A doctor who examined the baby after said that there was nothing anyone could have done to prevent the death of this precious one. Still, I could not shake the anxious feelings that came every time I thought of the grief that these parents experienced. I wondered many times if this could have been prevented if the birth had taken place in a hospital. Since it did not give me any peace pondering the possibilities, I would bury my feelings deep inside of me, so I could have some sense of peace in the last months of my pregnancy. My personal prayers became quite intense in asking the Lord for His guidance, wisdom, mercy, and grace as the day for the birth approached. Thank God I had a house full of children to keep me occupied in a good and productive way.

*   *

The sisters of the fellowship asked if they could be part of the birth and I agreed reluctantly. One part of me felt there was strength in numbers, yet the other part did not want the bottom part of my body to be exposed to so many eyes, while bringing forth a new baby into our family. On January 30, I started labour in earnest in the middle of the morning. The pains in my lower back the night before had forewarned me that I was in for the experience of a lifetime, having a homebirth with 2 elderly women as midwives and the sisters of the fellowship in attendance. As it was a Monday, the three older children were in school and were only going to be looked after for one night away from home, but the 2 youngest were going for a whole week. A flurry of activities preceded their exit from our home as I was getting things ready for them, strong labour preventing me from being sharp in my mind and fast in body.

*   *

Around 6:30 pm Mrs. M told me to get in bed as I was bleeding quite heavy. I promised that I was almost ready to do so. By 7 o'clock I laid down in bed with the knowledge that everything was in reasonable order for my little one to arrive. The bleeding did not stop but increased with every labour pain. The sisters started to arrive by this time. I do not remember how many there were, but they were standing in a half a circle around the room. Michael was on my left side on his knees and supported me with a strong arm. I knew he was quite nervous and tried his best to hide it, to comfort me. After a couple of pushes, by 9:30 pm our little boy was born. Michael was overjoyed that it was all over and hugged me tight. I laid back and praised the Lord with a great feeling of accomplishment. My husband cut the cord and I expected to have this baby in my arms at any moment. There was no cry or even the slightest noise, which was strange! There was an ominous feeling in the atmosphere as the sisters were praying, not praising.

"What's the matter?" I asked.

"Ahh, sister Corine the baby is not breathing."

"Hold him upside down Mom and smack his little bum!" I urged

"We did that already, but he's not breathing."

I leaned on my elbows and looked at a little blue-grey baby at the end of my bed. I had no idea of how much time it had been since he was born. The prayers of the sisters became louder, and a feeling of fear was now in the air. Later I learned that more than 5 minutes had passed. Deep in my belly arose a rebuke! A heavenly language with great authority came out of my mouth and as I spoke, I pointed to my little boy with an outstretched arm. Right at the moment I pointed my finger to him, he took a deep breath and started to cry! There was a release of tension and most of us wept!

* *

There was such joy in the camp and with hearts of thanksgiving we were praising the Lord until well after the baby was weighed, suckled, dressed, and cradled in the arms of those present. We named him Jeremiah Elisha. This baby did not leave me that night as he slept on my tummy. His tiny ear close to my heart, so there was no interruption of the comforting beat, the constant sound that was part of his development in the months prior to his birth.

*   *

I went before the Lord, asking Him why this birth was so traumatic. He showed me that I had placenta previa. Since the bleeding started with labour, it was most likely a partial cover of or at the edge of the cervix. We had a healthy baby otherwise and were so thankful. This baby slept the first week of his life on his mother's chest, nursing often and being cradled and loved by family and members of our newfound fellowship. Then he was put in the bassinet that was used for all the previous children but he was not sleeping well after that change. I believe in swaddling my babies, it is like being safe in the womb, warm and not much room to move. No matter how I wrapped him in the receiving blanket, he got his little arms out in no time. He kept swinging them around his little face and cried a lot. Since it was in the middle of winter, there was no way to walk outside with him in his pram, which I did a lot with my other children who were born in other seasons. I placed him in the porch, which was cool, but placed a warm water bottle in his back and on the back of his legs, covering the pram with a light blanket. He was truly as snug as a bug in that space. He slept 3 hours in a row when he was there, but when night came, I brought him in, and the crying and restlessness started again.

*   *

I talked to Jesus about the situation and asked what the matter was for this baby to be so calm outside but so aggravated up in his bedroom. After about 2 months, something like a light went off in my head and received a word: 'allergies'. Then I asked what Jeremiah was allergic to. Environment! There was something in our room he was reacting to. I did not have to search for long as old wood has mold spores imbedded in its grooves. The whole ceiling of our bedroom was raw wood, as it was an old farmhouse. I kept him downstairs after that and we all slept much better.

*   *

Not until after we had a visit to the Netherlands when Jeremiah was 11, he was tested to see what he was reacting to. Feathers, wool, dogs and cats and mold were just some of the things he tested positive for. Poor little guy, many household items in Holland are made from the real stuff. Feather pillows and woolen carpets were in most houses. He was quite a mess, dark circles under his eyes and always teary. I would call him: 'Jeremiah the weeping prophet'.

*   *

When we were living in another house and we had a little space with uncovered wood from the roof in one bedroom, he could not sleep there as he became wheezy and uncomfortable. After he was tested, he would visit our doctor once a week before school for allergy shots, but he did not feel good after the injections and after a while stopped going. I found someone who sold Aloe Vera juice and started him on garlic and parsley tablets. At least I knew that he was getting stronger, and the treatment was calming the immune system. In time he was not reacting to all the allergens anymore. I believe the Lord for supernatural healing, but until that takes place, I will use what He has provided through natural or medical means.

There is a time for everything, but for us to wait upon the Lord for healing, we sure need His grace and practice patience.

18

THE WASHING MACHINE SAGA

While we were living in Newmarket, we had Mom and Dad M with their son John, my sister from the Netherlands and our family together at the old farmhouse. In a household that big, there is lots of food that needs to be prepared. I loved cooking, no problem there, and lots of laundry, a bit of a problem there!

* *

The wringer washer we had went on the blink and Dad and Michael went to the Saturday Stouffville market to see if they could find one for not too much money. They came home with another wringer washer. It was in good working condition at that time but only for a couple of months. When it was not working anymore Michael and Dad went to a Richmond Hill bargain store for another machine. They brought home another second hand, or maybe even third hand wringer-washer. It did not matter to me what kind of machine it was as long as I could keep up with the amount of laundry that accumulated in just a couple of days. Because the other machine broke down in the midst of doing laundry,

I had an enormous amount of washing to do with our newly acquired appliance.

So I plugged in the machine, filled it up with hot water and soap, added the first load, the 'white' wash, and looked for the start button for the agitator to begin the wash cycle. I could not find any! I looked high and low on this machine, unplugged the cord from the wall outlet, and plugged it in again. I could hear the hum of the motor but did not see a handle or knob for the agitator to be initiated. I became worried that I could not get the laundry done and sat down on a chair, put my head in my hands and cried out in desperation to the Lord!

As I closed my eyes and just sitting there wondering what to do next, the Lord gave me a vision. In that vision I saw a hand of an angel with a white sleeve over his arm, making a downward movement on top of the agitator. I jumped up and put my hand down on the agitator and it started its rotation!

I danced around, praising the Lord as my washing machine was doing its job. I was elated that our Lord, who is such a big God, was interested in our everyday activities and as he has promised never to leave us nor forsake us, He was right there in my need to finish my laundry!!

What a Savior we serve.

Well, that washing machine lasted until our baby Jeremiah was 2 months old, and this time we went to a department store in the Mall just across from our home. Michael and I picked out the most basic 'automatic' machine as the price played a huge role in our choice. The new washing machine was scheduled to be delivered on Friday March 31, 1978. It had to come from the warehouse in Toronto, as there was no sale on any of the floor-models. We were OK with that.

The day before the machine was to arrive; I had all the

laundry in piles by colors and was on my last couple of cotton diapers. I did not buy any disposables because when I used them on our oldest boy, he got a big rash. We were counting on the new appliance to be there the next day, it did not concern me that I only a couple clean ones left.

* *

The day we expected our new washer, a huge snowstorm moved in from the south and blanketed the lower parts of Ontario. We woke up to a very white landscape that morning. We listened to the news and came to the realization that all of southern Ontario's traffic was ordered off the roads, as they were impassible. The accumulation was bad because it was not fluffy snow, but the heavy stuff, loaded with water and it was a about a foot and a half deep.

I called the department store immediately and they told me that there would be no delivery trucks going north from Toronto until maybe Monday or even Tuesday as their deliveries to all the stores would be backed up. I promptly started to cry as I felt so overwhelmed by the fact that we had laundry all over the place. Our kitchen floor was more looking like wall-to-wall dirty laundry, and I had no more clean diapers for my baby. The lady at Sears asked me why it was so important for me to have this washing machine delivered that day. I told her that our old machine had broken down 10 days before and the amount of laundry was depressing to say the least. Diapers were most needed and told her some just had to be washed by hand, and we ended the conversation.

Not even 10 minutes later we got a call back from her, telling us that they were going to load a floor model washing machine from their store onto a pick-up truck and since it was just across the road, they were confident that it would not have too many problems plowing through that snow to our house.

We were absolutely thrilled that they were trying to help us in this way. The appliance came not even 2 hours later, and what a surprise, it was their top-of-the-line washing machine. That sure turned my tears of frustration into tears of joy. That machine lasted for 25 years!!

* *

We serve such a big God. Never underestimate His care and thoughtfulness for you. These incidents increased our faith! We can read all kinds of nice poems about faith, but until you are experiencing His intervention and the benefit of seeing the Hand of God at work, you have something to hold onto and apply it in your future. That is the testimony that helps you overcome stumbling blocks and make them 'step-up' stones. In the most adverse situations to see the Hand of God at work is truly living in His Kingdom.

Have faith!

19

PASSPORT PROBLEMS

We came to Canada on an encouraging word from my Mom's sister who came to this country in 1948. She was the one that told us we did not have to wait for a house as there were plenty in Canada to rent or to buy. But my father also had a sister that emigrated in 1952. She lived in the Kingston area with her husband and 10 children. The one thing I wanted to do as soon as we had a chance was to go and visit that family.

* *

The year is 1966, so when you go and visit or even shop, you dress up! With our new, used 1960 light blue Ford sedan and certainly not comfortable travel attire we started the long trip from Thornhill to Kingston. My husband was wearing a nice light-colored herringbone sports jacket and I was in a pretty dress. It was a sunny day, and our clothes were not only warm for wear but also not easy for sitting in a car without air-conditioning. The jacket came off soon after we started our trip, and we had the windows wide open to feel the comforting breeze. When we arrived at the farmhouse in Bath, Ontario we quickly put the pieces of clothing on that had found their way on the back seat of our car while traveling.

* *

It was a wonderful feeling to connect with my aunt and her big family. We were welcomed with coffee, food and an immediate discovery trip around the farm. By this time, the sun was sure showing its strength and the dress jacket came off and was put on the back of a chair around the dining table. In the inside pocket Michael had his Swedish passport, and to this day I have wondered why that important piece of ID was not in a safe place at our home in Thornhill.

* *

Even though he was born and raised in Amsterdam his whole family was of Swedish nationality. Grandfather Emil Zacharias M was born in 1874 in a small seafaring community called Gavle, about one hour north of Stockholm. He was a sailor from a young age and joined the Merchant Marines. Certainly, he would have visited many European harbors, one of them being Rotterdam, where he met and married Michael's grandmother.

* *

The Dutch Nationality law before 1954 was such that if you, as a Dutch woman married a gentleman from another country you had no choice but take on your husband's nationality, and any children born out of that union would be citizens of the husband's country of origin, even when born and raised in the Netherlands. My father-in-law and his sister were Swedish while living in Holland. On the other side of this law is my uncle, who married a German lady, and she became a Dutch citizen. Michael's father, had to regularly get his Swedish citizenship papers updated to stay current and if not, he would become a displaced person. When my husband's Dad married, Maria van der P in 1942, she also became Swedish through marriage. All 4 children born in that union were Swedish citizens and the parents had to make sure that they stayed current.

* *

After World War II they tried to get their Dutch Citizenship as a family but were very discouraged when they found out it would cost them a small fortune to do so. There was hardly provision for a family to eat properly, leave alone having a large sum of money to become Dutch. When we came to Canada the Immigration Officer hand-wrote in my passport: '*Echtgenoot geen Nederlander*' translated: 'Husband not a Dutchman.' Must have been a big deal at that time.

* *

Since it was such a beautiful warm day when we visited my family, Michael's jacket was forgotten and left on the back of that chair in the dining room. We did not think about the passport in that inner pocket, but surely missed the jacket for going out for dinner or dancing. I phoned my aunt, and she would look after it until we visited again. It was a faraway place for us at that time and did not get back there until a couple of months later. Glad to have that important piece of clothing back, we realized much later that the passport was not in that jacket anymore.

We also found out that at Michael's 22nd birthday he

lost his Swedish nationality because he did not go to the Swedish consulate before the expiry date. When we phoned the Consulate, we received this information; He could get his status back if he stayed in Sweden for 2 years and then also served in their army. We did not give them any information about the loss of his passport as he could not have travelled on an expired citizenship anyway. My husband was now a displaced person. He could not travel outside of Canada, neither could he apply for Canadian citizenship as he did not have the proper papers. Thankfully, we still had the Landed Immigrant status, a tiny slip of paper to prove we landed in Montreal on the 28th of April 1966.

Future travels and visiting the home country again looked very bleak, as there was nothing we could do to change it. Once we became faithful followers of Christ, we did not even make it a prayer request. Busy with family life and a small business there was no thought of traveling, and if a thought would creep in, it was squashed immediately as there was no money for such a luxury.

* *

Next, amazing grace, truly amazing!

Ten years later the tide turned and in a very unexpected way. We were living in Newmarket at the time and received a phone call from the Dutch Consulate. It was concerning Michael's brother John. He was not well and had psychological problems all his life. Apparently, he had made his way to the USA by crossing the border somewhere in the south of the Prairies. The Consulate employee told us quite a story of John's travels. He was arrested because he was carrying a big knife and said that he was on his way to kill President Reagan. After having been taken into custody they found out that he lived in Canada but had a Dutch passport. How he ever became a Dutch citizen is still a mystery to this family. How long he was in jail in the US we do not know, but they did give him a choice; to be deported back to Canada or a trip to the Netherlands. John choose to be sent to Holland because he was wanted by the police of the town we lived in, for outstanding charges, all related to his illness.

* *

It was because of the deportation of one of its citizens back to home country that the Dutch Consulate contacted us. They also knew that he was a paranoid schizophrenic and needed to get some background information on his condition. I was speaking with this gentleman for quite some time, and I asked how John had a Dutch passport while the rest of the family was Swedish. He did not have an answer for this, in addition he did not believe that the rest of the family had Swedish passports, as they were all born and raised in Amsterdam. I then told him that not all the family members were Swedish any longer, as my husband lost that citizenship on his 22nd birthday in 1966. He asked a couple more questions about my husband's teenage years back home. When I told him that he served in the Army he responded with a very stern voice and said:

"That is impossible!"

"Why would that be impossible, Sir?"

"A person having a Swedish or any other nationality would not be drafted into the Dutch army."

"Sir, I have pictures of him in his army uniform with other soldiers".

"No, no, a Swedish person cannot serve in the Dutch army."

"But he did, he really did. Would you like it if I send these pictures to you?" Then it was quiet at the other end of the phone.

"Just a moment please, I'll be right back."

"Ma'am, if he served in the Army, he gained Dutch citizenship through serving the Queen."

"What? What was that you said?"

The words he was saying were racing through my brain, wanting to understand and see the future for traveling in these couple of seconds.

"You mean he actually was Dutch since he served in the Army?"

Michael was standing close, and I relayed the news as I received it. Then that gentleman gave us some instructions what to do to get the papers in order. Pictures were to be taken and send to Amsterdam to receive a birth certificate and proof of citizenship. After a couple of weeks, we received the important papers that were necessary to prepare for a Dutch passport. There was such a feeling of celebration in our household and I certainly had a permanent smile on my face.

* *

Once the passport was in Michael's hand, we could not stop thanking the Lord for His goodness. We did not have any hope of ever traveling out of the country together, but the Lord had made a way already in 1963 when Michael received a notice from the Dutch government to come in for testing, before he was drafted. If my husband was aware at that time that he did not have to answer to report for duty because he was not a Dutch citizen, he would have certainly made good use of that information and declined the draft legally.

Looking back to that time, we are so thankful that he made his entry into the Dutch army on the 4th of March 1964 and served the Dutch Queen for 18 months.

The Lord foreknows our steps and affairs, even before we commit our lives to him.

"Before I formed you in the womb, I knew you, before you were born I set you apart" Jeremiah. 1:5

We are in awe of how He works with time and circumstance to turn a bleak situation into a glorious one.

20

A PLACE TO LIVE AND A PLACE TO STAY

The bakery floor in Aurora was not in compliance with the health department. By their standards, the floor was to be non-porous. It was covered with slats of wood and we were given a certain time to bring it up to the acceptable standard. The owner was not willing to spend about $20,000 to improve the floor, so Michael looked for another place to set up the bakery. They found a unit in Barrie. It needed some major changes and extra equipment to be able to keep the production line running smoothly, but that was doable.

* *

The 2-year lease on the farmhouse in Newmarket had come to an end. Michael's brother had sold the property that he and his wife owned in the Netherlands and he gifted Mom and Dad a certain amount of money for a down payment to buy a house. As the new bakery unit was already in Barrie, the search was on for a big house in that village, for the whole family.

A 2-story house was found just in walking distance from the bakery. The upstairs was a self-contained apartment. It was decided that Mom and Dad take the upstairs and Michael and his family occupy the downstairs. There were 2 bedrooms, so we had to fit some bunk beds in the kid's bedroom. In time it was a bedroom for 8 children. 3 bunk beds, 2 highboy dressers and one wide dresser were in that room which was no bigger than 12 x 13 feet. In the middle of the room we placed a fold-up cot for Jerusha. A trundle bed, without the mattress, full of Lego, was pushed neatly underneath one bunk bed set when the kids were at school or sleeping.

* *

When we lived in Keswick, we were told that we had to move because the owners wanted to move back in their house. I asked the Lord for us be able to just stay in one place, so our children did not have to go to a different school every 2 years. He provided that through the house Mom and Dad were able to buy.

* *

Jeremiah was 6 months old when we moved into our new place which had a huge backyard. Michael strung up a clothesline immediately and there were enough trees to enjoy sitting outside in the shade. Since Jeremiah had slept so well outside in his pram in Newmarket, I had my baby underneath a tree, partly in the sun to get some vitamin D, while I got the house in order. In the first week of our move he was crying quite a bit, most likely because I was so busy. Thankfully, the schoolyear had come to an end and I had the older children to help me. Shortly after our move, Jeremiah was outside and sharing his grievance of being alone in the pram, with the neighborhood. I checked him often, making sure he was dry and safe. I said to him:

"Well little man, you just have to cry yourself to sleep," and walked back to the house. Since he was just fed, I was confident that there was no stress, but he just wanted to be held. My hands were full, and I had to finish some necessary tasks. About 5 minutes later the crying stopped and I just wanted to check that he was sleeping. Walking outside I saw my new next-door neighbor rocking the pram! I had not yet met her and was surprised she felt comfortable enough to step into our backyard and rock my baby. I made my acquaintance with her and had a short conversation about the neighborhood. In the meantime, she kept rocking the pram, which made me laugh. I told her that she had put the little guy to sleep and that he would be fine now. She wore a beautiful sari and looked so classic with part of the sari covering her beautiful dark hair. From that moment I knew she was not only going to be a good neighbor but also a good friend. After that I was often invited over to her house, which when I had tea with her, always felt free to talk about my faith and she about hers. Our children played together, and I had the privilege of looking after her boy and girl a few times. We made sure when on vacation that we checked each other's houses for mail and that the plants were watered.

* *

One morning another neighbor came to borrow a cup of sugar. She had knocked on the front door. You had to step up onto a bit of a cement patch to reach the door, but she had gone back down on the grass. I must have looked very tall to her as she was of short stature and was standing much lower than I. Bringing the sugar to her, I reached down to give it and noticed that she looked quite pale.

"Are you OK? You're not looking so good."

"I am having such a bad headache" was her reply.

"Can I pray for you?"

She looked a bit curious but agreed to prayer. I bent down, took her hands with the cup in it and held them while I prayed a short prayer in the name of Jesus and touched with my forehead, her forehead.

"It's gone!" she said in surprise.

I told her to have a good rest of the day.

In later years, our next-door neighbors had their house raised to add a basement and extra bedrooms. It took some time before it was all done. The last thing was the extra bedrooms and the roof extension over that area. My neighbor came early in the morning before the roof was to be extended. All the bedding had to find a dry place as we expected rain all that day. She asked if she could store them in our garage. Of course, we allowed her to do so! I said to her that I was going to pray and ask the Lord to keep the rain away from us. When she came to pick up the blankets in the evening, I reminded her of the prayer and said:

"Look, the Lord answered! It rained all around, but nor here." It was so good to see the roof to the addition come to completion in such a short time.

* *

It is God who will draw with His goodness and all that is expected from us is to be is a light, loving and kind, even if we do not see results of our actions of evangelism or prayer.

"Let us not become weary in doing good, for at the proper time we will reap a harvest if we do not give up" Galatians 6:9

21

FACING DEATH

After the bakery moved to Barrie from Aurora, my husband was on the hunt for some bakery equipment. Second hand was best as the price would be affordable but what he found was quite some kilometers north from Sudbury. A flatbed truck was rented, and Michael was going to bring the equipment to the new unit. He was looking at about 3 ½ hours travel up to Capreol. He had some helpers to dismantle the oven and other bakery items from a discontinued bakery there.

Shortly after Jeremiah's first birthday, I found that I was with child once more. By this time both Michael and I had resigned to the fact that there might be more children in our future.

"3 Children are a heritage from the LORD, offspring a reward from him. 4 Like arrows in the hands of a warrior are children born in one's youth. 5 Blessed is the man whose quiver is full of them". Psalm 127:3-5

Planning how everything would fit in our cramped quarters was not in our vision yet. We were not going to tell anyone until I was about halfway when I would start showing that a new baby was going to join the family. Mom M was told of course, being family and my confidante. When Michael went up north to get the equipment, I was 13 weeks into the pregnancy. He kissed me goodbye that Friday and promised it would not take much more than a couple of days before he would be back home. Once supper was done that evening and the little ones tucked in bed, I noticed something was not in order. I had started to bleed. That was alarming as I had a miscarriage before Stephanie, and I was a bit of an emotional mess after that. This time we were serving the Lord and knew He was my Healer and a very present help in trouble. I went upstairs to visit Mom, to ask for prayer. I wanted to be in faith and needed to have someone stand with me. Mom told me that it would be ok, maybe just some spotting. After I went back downstairs feeling alone in my concern that something was amiss. As my husband was not home, I poured out my heart to God, and felt His love and protection.

* *

Saturday was a difficult day as the weekly shopping had to be done and the house cleaned. The children all had their chores, and I went grocery shopping. By evening time I had released my concern and the baby inside of me, to God. Sunday was better as the fellowship would gather to praise the Lord. At least there was a lot of distraction and I would be able to share with my sisters what was going on and not feel alone in my sadness. Sunday night before retiring I asked Jesus to show me about this baby that I had already connected to. He gave me a dream! There was a lot in the dream, but one thing stood out: Jesus was holding a little girl on His arm, with long blond hair.

"She's with me".

I woke up and wept, but the dream was so comforting that I could go on with my day without being overtaken by grief. I had a hard time getting over my first miscarriage, like walking in a grey cloud, grieving over what could have been and was no more. I never thought that one could have such a hard time with the loss of a baby in the womb, just 3 months in its growth.

This time was different as Jesus showed me that it was a girl, and she was with Him. Still the pain was real like a rugburn on my heart. I kept giving the situation to the Lord and prayed for peace.

*   *

Tuesday morning at 6 am I felt labour pains. I knew I was going to lose the fetus. I felt such energy just like when a baby was going to be born at full term. I pulled the sheets of the children's beds and started to wash them. Mom came down to find out how I was doing. Surprised at the energy I was showing, she told me to take it easy. I had a coffee with her and around 10 o'clock felt to push. In the bathroom I held a tiny grey baby in my hand. I cried as I checked her out. Everything was so small but perfect, tiny little fingers and toes. The mouth, eyes and ears were minute but all there. What caused this baby's death, I wondered, but did not want to give it much thought as it only saddened me. I committed it to the ground in our backyard. She is with Jesus, I kept saying.

*   *

Mom insisted that I go to bed, but I said that I just wanted to be on the couch. On my way to the living room, I stepped over Jerusha's blanket and I started to hemorrhage, like a floodgate was opened. Good thing it was over a blanket as it would have totally ruined our carpet. I packed myself with my housecoat and did go to my bed. I did not stop hemorrhaging and Mom kept putting clean sheets underneath me and putting the bloody ones in the bathtub. After about half an hour I went unconscious. I remember coming back with Mom praying over me and rebuking the devil!

"You're not going to take her life! She has children to look after", is what I remember.

At that time Karen from another town came over for a visit. She saw what was happening, put 1 year old Jeremiah in a stroller and walked as fast as she could to the bakery, where others were working. She told them that there was a great need in our household. A sister of the fellowship that I had great respect for was called. She said that she could not come over until her daughter came back from school; that would be around 3:30 and then had to make her way to our home. In the meantime, Mom and Karen changed sheets and prayed. I kept going in and out of consciousness. At one-point Mom said firmly:

"Corine, you cannot fall asleep!"

I was so tired and gladly would have just given up and gone to sleep. Amazingly, I was not thinking of the repercussions if I did go to sleep. In my mind I would just wake up after a little snooze. Mom saw how I was convulsing and then lay very still. She kept talking loud in my ear, but it sounded like it came from a faraway place. I struggled to stay with it. I had clarity at one point and asked the Lord if I was to die. I asked Mom too, as somehow, I had to have permission to just let go. Mom said that the sister from the fellowship would be with us soon and told me again that I had lots to live for. Slipping in and out of consciousness with Mom's voice calling me back time and time again, I waited for that sister to give me the OK to go to Jesus. Around 4 pm she arrived. She was standing in the doorway of the bedroom, and I asked:

"Am I going to die?"

"Corine" she said in a forceful way: "We are to be the glory of the Lord in THIS earth!"

With all I could muster I said:

"OK, then I want to go to the bathroom".

Really? Did that come out of my mouth? I did not even feel an urge to empty my bladder. But three sisters and Mom where ready to haul me up and get me going.

Somehow, I got my feet on the floor and stood up straight, raised my hands to the Lord and praised Him! I thanked and glorified the Lord in the loudest voice possible for me at that time. Then I fainted! When I came to, I thanked Him for keeping me alive to look after the ones He had entrusted to me. I was told later that they thought that I was kind of hallucinating, but not so! I was clear in my mind and knew Jesus had touched me.

The sister from the fellowship and Karen left, but Mom looked after me with something to drink and started supper for the children and Dad. Later that evening, Mom and Dad and others sat around my bed and filled the room with songs of praise.

* *

I missed my husband dearly through this ordeal and had no idea that he was stuck in Parry Sound. The flat-bed truck full of bakery equipment broke down and had to be repaired, which would take a couple of days. Michael stayed behind while the helpers hitched a ride home. There were no cell phones then, so we got the news once the guys came back. Michael came home later that week and once he informed me of what had happened, felt sorry he could not have been home as a support for his family.

* *

The next day I had Mother M from the 'Fellowship' to help me, but I was quite strong. I even bathed the little ones but had to be careful not to get up too quick, or shake my head, as my vision would catch up in slow motion with the movement of my head. I was amazed at the energy I felt in the following days to look after the household. My hands were white for 14 days but after that period I saw pink starting to show on my fingertips. I was on my way to total health once again.

* *

A couple of months later I was pregnant again. The due date was the 28th of March 1980. It was the end of June 1979 and deep down I was anxious. I did not show it outwardly and just prayed and gave my concerns to God. I put my situation on the altar and then took it back almost immediately, worrying that I might go through what happened in May, again. Even with the amazing recovery I had experienced, which was nothing short of a miracle, I had no peace. I prayed earnestly to Jesus and asked for a healthy baby. In August, the Lord gave me a dream. In the dream I gave birth to a baby girl on the 23rth of September. I woke up and said:

"Oh no!!", but felt no fear.

My mind was not racing, my heart calm.

"Well Lord what is that all about?" I asked in my mind.

Then came clarity: September....the 9th month. That made my heart sing, and I praised the Lord in my heavenly language.

*   *

Not until I gave birth to Naomi on the 23rth of March, I knew it was a prophetic dream back in August. I encouraged my daughter Naomi in the Lord with the words that the baby before her was destined for heaven and therefore made the way for her to be born and to be sold out to Jesus, being a bright light in a darkening world. She is a firebrand for God!

22

NAOMI

Quite often around Christmas there seems to be a flu or bad cold making its way around our family, and the year that Naomi was born was no exception.

She was born in March 1980, our seventh child. She was about 9 months old when she became sick with a severe cold. Little ones do not have the immune system yet to fight off a nasty respiratory virus and sometimes a secondary infection can be detrimental to their health.

*   *

We were in this Christian Cult already for 6 years and survived some injuries and illnesses that had affected the members over those years without consulting a doctor. To go to a medical facility to seek the help of the medical profession was like a death sentence in the spirit. According to the leader, the Lord would not look favorably on us and we would certainly not get His blessings on our health and family. Surely this conviction was what set the group apart from other Christian fellowships. So, when our little one became sick, I was on my knees seeking the Lord, which is a good thing! My husband, myself and the children would pray for her to get better every day. But days went by and she did not show any improvement.

* *

A playpen was put close to the wall in the living room away from any doorway and I hung sheets around the sides so no draft would touch her. I still nursed her and did that often to get enough fluids into her as she would not eat any solids. When I had that little head close to my skin, I knew the fever was high, the only way to tell as I did not have a thermometer in my possession. Her breathing was laboured, and I had the feeling that she had a touch of pneumonia. At night I sat close to her and prayed and sang songs while playing the guitar. I only knew the basic chords, but you can sing quite a few songs strumming these simple chords.

* *

Looking after the older children in the day and being watchful at night was very tiring. I would snooze a bit here and there even in the daytime when the children were at school and Jeremiah who was 2 years older than Naomi went for an afternoon nap; but not getting a good night's sleep was wearing on me. In a situation like that it is hard not to get discouraged. One of the women of the fellowship saw the need and suggested she would come and stay with Naomi one night, for me to be able to get refreshed with a full night sleep. I agreed, as I knew I would not last much longer without a good rest, but not to be close to my sick little daughter was also causing me a bit of anxiety.

* *

It was agreed that this sister-in-the Lord would come around 11 pm and stay until the older children were off to school. Before she arrived that night, I prayed fervently that the Lord would touch our Naomi and to heal her lungs. I was pleading the Blood of Jesus over her, and then I had this picture in my mind of a red dome covering our house.

I prayed that the Blood of Jesus would be over our home just like that impression. Around 11 that evening my rescuer came in.

"Guess what I saw Corine, guess what I saw?!"
she said before taking of her coat and a bit out of breath.

I was curious, as she was so excited at something she saw. It was night so what could be seen except maybe a critter running across the street?

* *

Our street runs down from a road that overlooks the city of Barrie and part of the Kempenfelt Bay, so as you come from that height you look down on the houses of only 3 streets that were in that valley at that time. There were a lot of low bushes and brush, but no tall trees obscuring that view.

"As I was coming around the corner and turning onto your street, I saw a red covering over your house like a dome!"

She was gesturing with her hands and making a rounding motion over an imagined item. Just as I had the picture in my mind when I pleaded the Blood of Jesus. I shared my experience with her in an exiting voice. We hugged and praised the Lord for His goodness. What a confirmation that Jesus was in control. What a calming effect it had on my whole being. I had a good sleep that night. He looks at your heart; He sees your love and dedication to Him. He rewards those that diligently seek Him, even if that journey takes you through some not so sound and even false doctrine.

* *

Naomi got better from that night on, her breathing was already so much clearer the next morning. She had lost some weight and strength, but her Daddy was fasting for a couple of weeks and instead of feeding himself, he was feeding her. She accepted every bite he offered her and about a week later you could see the color return in her little face.

As she turned one year old in March there was no sign in her body that she had gone through a severe illness. I thanked and praised Jesus that no matter where your walk is in Him, He truly is one who rewards, and will according to the scriptures work everything for good for those that love Him and are called according to His purpose.

23

SALT

I t is such an important mineral!
There is evidence that man used salt as early as 6000 years ago. It was highly prized and used for trading among the ancient Egyptians, Greeks, Byzantines, Hittites, Hebrews and Romans. The word 'salary' is derived from 'salarium' which means salt. In ancient Rome the soldiers were paid out in part by a portion of salt. If the Roman soldiers did not want their senior officers to think that 'they were not worth their salt'; they worked extra hard.

When we are at work or do some strenuous sport in hot weather, it is important to drink water with some salt, because when we sweat, we lose salt naturally through the pores of our skin. Our hearts would not be working properly if we did not have the right amount of salt in our blood. When we are constantly low on salt, our brains cannot function, and confusion will set in. *(Dr. Mercola)* Hyponatremia is a condition in which the body has abnormal low amounts of sodium in the blood. It is quite dangerous, could cause a coma, seizures and even death. *(Mayo Clinic)*

* *

Salt has a very purifying effect on skin. In times past, when a child or an adult had skin conditions such as eczema or skin conditions that were hard to treat, they were suggested to go to ocean beaches. Sun and salty water healed many stubborn conditions. There are many spas around the Dead Sea as the salinity combined with other important minerals in that seawater is well known for healing the skin.

Without the seasoning of salt in our food, it would be a bland meal. Preservation and curing of foods is still done with salt. It is important in making pickles, meat jerky and there would be no sauerkraut without the use of copious amounts of salt layered in sliced cabbage. Salt licks have to be available for farm animals. Even on the bison reservation north of Winnipeg, we saw great salt blocks to ensure the animals received enough of this mineral in their diet. Maybe our God caused the sea to contain 3.5 % salts, mostly sodium, so we will never run out of it.

* *

"You are the salt of the earth. But if the salt loses its saltiness, how can it be made salty again? It is no longer good for anything, except to be thrown out and trampled underfoot. Matthew 5:13

I was wondering how salt could lose its flavour. When you dissolve salt in fluid, it disappears. How can it be trampled under the feet of men? In Jesus' time the salt most likely that was used for flavoring was impure, more like rock salt, with some plant material and sand mixed in the salt crystals. Once the bag that contained salt was used until the salt was dissolved, it was not good for flavoring anymore and thrown on the street and walked on by men. When

Jesus said: "You are the salt of the earth" He pointed out how important a true follower of Christ is. We are to be salty Christians. To lose its saltiness can also mean you can water the salt down. When we do not adhere to the teachings of Christ and conform to the world and its norms, we become watered-downed Christians, still believing that Jesus Christ is the Son of God, even believing that He died for us, but not following or obeying the principles of His teaching while He walked this earth, all contained in the gospels.

In the Old Testament salt symbolizes purity, perfection, wisdom, hospitality durability and fidelity. When Jesus made that statement about being the salt of the earth, He referred to all that was written before He was born.

* *

Salt is also a healer, and my experience with this wonderful mineral happened in 1982. In August of that year another baby was expected. This one was our 8th child. It was an uncomfortable hot summer and I found it to be a very trying time with a bulging belly and looking after the other children and canning. Air-conditioning was a luxury that we could not afford, but we had enough fans to keep the air circulating. It kept us somewhat comfortable.

* *

The aging mothers of the fellowship were once again the midwives who would assist me in bringing this baby in the world. It was our responsibility to have everything ready for the wonderful and at times scary event of bringing forth a baby at home instead of at the hospital. One of the items we were to have at hand was a shoelace to tie of the umbilical cord before it was cut. My husband tried to find a flat shoelace as that was the best, but all he could find were the round ones. Shoelaces that have a flat cross-section are generally easier to tie and stay tied better that those that are round. All other items that were needed for a homebirth were under a sheet, ready to be used once that baby made his arrival known by a strong and healthy cry.

* *

Benjamin was born in the evening without any complications. There was a lot of rejoicing and laughter. A very tired but happy Mom saw how Dad cut the cord. The baby was wrapped in a homemade receiving blanket and given to me to hold, cuddle and nurse immediately. The household quieted down soon after the birth. The smaller children were among friends for a couple of days and the excitement of a new baby tired out the older ones, so to have them in their beds in good time, was no problem. It was a wonderful thing to have 2 mothers busying themselves in taking care of everything from meals to laundry. They enjoyed looking after the baby and I gave them that liberty as I knew that soon enough, I would be back on my feet from dawn to dusk caring for the household on my own. The home was looked after, and I enjoyed just nursing Benjamin, reading and knitting without interruptions.

* *

About two days later, I was sitting on the end of my bed when Mrs. M handed me the baby to be fed. I smelled something like a dirty diaper, but babies that are nursed will have stools smelling like buttermilk. It confused me and asked her what was going on. She explained that the cord had not been tied off tight enough; it had still been bleeding for about a day. I was shocked and immediately uncovered his belly to see for myself how serious it was. Mrs. M said that she was to blame as she did not have a strong enough grip to tie the shoelace properly. The bleeding had given life to the umbilical stump, instead of dying off it was as big as 10 mm without any signs of drying. After the discovery of the bleeding, she had tied another shoelace underneath the first one, with both mothers making sure it was done right this time. The smell was not pretty, and I went to prayer, petitioning the Lord for healing and wisdom on how to deal with this in-the-face problem.

* *

In staying with the requirements of notation of a live birth and registration with the government, we would make an appointment with a physician for a 6-week baby-well checkup. Even though the visit to the doctor was still 5 weeks away, my stomach was having butterflies as I was anticipating questions about the 10 mm high belly button. It looked nothing like a button but more like a cylinder of skin, on top of the baby's belly. As I had nowhere else to go but to God, I asked Jesus what I could do, or for the Lord to have it miraculously disappear.

Not that it is the norm in how I asked for answers, but I was moved to close my eyes, turn the Bible upside down, twirl it around a couple of times and turn it around again. Then I opened it and pointed to a spot on that particular page, my eyes still closed. It was upside down, but I held my finger on that scripture and was amazed at the direction it gave.

"*On the day you were born your cord was not cut, nor were you washed with water to make you clean, nor were*

you rubbed with salt or wrapped in cloths." Ezekiel 16:4
SALT!!

I was a firm believer in using saltwater to gargle when one had a sore throat. Soak a wound in a saline solution to disinfect the site and wash off a scraped knee with a weaker solution so it will not sting. A finger with an imbedded sliver would get an overnight treatment of a saline soaked cotton ball to draw out the sliver. I called it the 'poor man's medicine'.

As I was familiar with the benefits of saltwater, I felt to make a slightly stronger solution and rubbed this on the umbilical stump, every time he needed a change of diaper. An amazing thing happened: a thin layer of the skin sloughed off as I rubbed the salty water on it. I realized that this solution was ensuring that the skin did not heal the area but kept it soft but not open. Benjamin was never bothered by this treatment, so I knew it was not stinging or hurting him.

*   *

The day that I had to make a visit to the doctor arrived, and even though there was still a visible stump of about 3 mm I did not feel anxious anymore. God was in control. The doctor wrote on the record that Benjamin was a healthy 6-week-old baby, and that he had a slight umbilical hernia. No questions were asked, and I did not volunteer any information on why it was not a hernia. I went home rejoicing and continued the treatment until there was no more elevation in that area. This boy has one of the best-looking bellybuttons of all our children. To this day I have used salt for cleansing and treating minor injuries. It brings me back with a thankful heart to the time that the Lord instructed me to use this mineral for His glory on a small child.

24

SAMUEL

1984 proved to be quite a busy year. Our 9th child was expected at the end of April. My mother from Holland was expected to be at the birth of this baby, as she was not able to be present at Jeremiah, Naomi, or Benjamin's birth. She so desired to be at one of my homebirths. It was agreed with Mom M. that since John, Michael's brother was not living with Mom and Dad at that time, his bedroom would provide a place for my Mom to sleep in a proper bed. After the 2nd night in that bedroom, she told me that she could not sleep up there. She said it was like something was sitting on her chest and she had a hard time breathing. We had a pull-out couch in the living room and made that bed for her to see if she could sleep better there. She slept soundly. Amazing how an extra body fitted in a house already bulging on all sides. I must agree that it was a very pleasant time with my Mom. She was not as overbearing as she was on previous visits and busied herself with ironing and knitting beside cleaning the dishes. I still had to finish dressing the basinet with new material, in the last week before the baby's expected day of birth. I mostly sewed at night when the children were in bed and Michael was resting on the couch. The night before the baby was born was no different, and just before midnight it was finished. I was pleased with the result and made the little bed ready before I crawled in my own, tired but glad it was for all in order for the little one to join our family. That was 2 am, and labour started immediately and strong. Quite early that day the children went upstairs to have Dad M. take care of them while Mom M and my own Mom were my midwives. I got some baby clothes together, and a homemade receiving blanket with blue colors.

My Mom said: "You think it's a boy?"

"Yes Mom, I believe we are going to have another little guy."

I trusted that Dad upstairs had everything in control and had great peace to give myself over to the task at hand. Michael, Mom M and my Mom were near me.

Dad M had to see the bigger ones off to school and keep the little ones close. Just as the school bus stopped at our driveway, Samuel was born. A good healthy cry signalled his arrival and the children wanted to see the baby before going to school. Dad ran out to the bus and asked the driver if he could wait a couple of minutes as a baby was just born at the house. He graciously agreed and as soon as the children had welcomed their new brother, they ran into the bus.

Samuel was a school-bus stopper!

*   *

The next day I was nursing him in my bedroom, and I poured out my thanksgiving to the God. It was a peaceful and good experience. The Lord spoke to my heart and said that this child will be the one that is going to look after

Michael and myself in our old age. I kept that in my heart as I would not put that kind of pressure on any of the children.

*   *

Mom and Dad M. moved to another village that year and we were able to purchase the house from them. We had 9 children at that time and the upstairs apartment became 4 bedrooms. It took some renovating as the kitchen upstairs had to be a bedroom for our two oldest boys. The room that had belonged to Michael's brother John needed some fresh paint and a new carpet. As we were working in that room, we had the same experience as my Mom a couple of months earlier. We had a hard time breathing there. Michael and I realized that it was housing an evil spirit and we went to prayer, opened the window, and commanded it to leave. We told it that this is a house of those that are washed in the Blood of Jesus and no devil could stay. Immediately we could breathe without any obstructions. God's provision for us to live free from the oppression of the enemy was won by the sacrifice of Jesus Christ some 2000 years ago.

*   *

The first night that each slept in their own bedroom was not a very restful one. The younger ones had problems being without all the others in one bedroom. But that did not last too long as they all appreciated their own space. After so many years it was a wonderful feeling to be able to run a household with some extra space. The previous children's bedroom became a front room with some much-needed closet space for shoes, boots, coats, and other items as we did not have a basement. Our bedroom downstairs became a dining room. The laundry room was in the garage. One had to walk outside to access it and in winter it was super cold and worrisome that the appliance might freeze. Our sons and my husband closed off a portion of the garage and made it part of the house, creating a laundry room that stayed warm and dry. The wall that separated the living room and kitchen was removed with the help of some members of the group and a wood burning stove was installed. The old furnace was removed as I could not handle the smell when that old thing would start burning oil. Little by little it became a house that all treasured until they left to be on their own.

I felt so blessed finding a space for the things that we needed, to keep a large family operating smoothly. For 40 years we lived in that house. Many memories are attached to that place. Half of our children have not known any other place to live in but this special piece of property, until they went out to find their own.

*   *

About 30 years later when we were ready to sell the house as it was way to big for us, empty nesters, we asked our children if any of them had a desire to buy the place. Samuel came forward with an offer to buy it. He was planning to tear down the old one and build a new house in its place. He also suggested that we would have a place like an in-law apartment on the side of their new house. What the Lord spoke to my heart so many years ago is coming to pass as I am writing this account.

His promises are yea and amen!

25

THE BARRIE TORNADO

Friday the 31st of May 1985 was a warm day. The winds were quite strong, but we did not mind, it felt like the tropics. Warm breezes were surrounding us, so clothes that were hung out on the clothesline dried very quickly, a busy Mom welcomed that! I had washed some windows, in particular the kitchen window that faced the north, it always had lots of handprints and finger marks on it as it had a counter-like structure underneath, that served as a telephone table. The windows were the old slider kind, four windows; the one set in the back overlapping another about 3 inches, and then for an element of insulation the same in the front, with clips to fasten each set. For some reason I had put only one set in and had left the other set on the floor underneath the window, just a little to the left side. The laundry was taken in before the children returned from school and I had prepared snacks for them as 3 of them had paper routes and were to be out of the door almost as soon as they arrived home.

* *

A week before something happened that was truly orchestrated by God, I am sure of this. Joshua, 11 at that time, had the paper route on our street and the one that ran parallel to it. Soon after he had finished his route, one of the customers called, wondering where his newspaper was. I queried Josh, and he said that he had delivered a paper there. We always had some extra newspapers, so he delivered one there immediately. After a couple of minutes another call with the same problem: no paper at their house either. After we solved that problem, the Newspaper company called us that they had received various complaints about not receiving their newspaper. This time we sat Joshua down and wanted to know why they had not received their paper. He kept a straight face and told me that he had delivered them all.

A little later we received another call from the Examiner. As they themselves delivered papers to the customers who had called in to their office, they found the missing papers. A stack of them were in the ditch! Josh was in trouble! The result was that he was not delivering newspapers in the next week, and therefore the money that was to be collected would go to Stephanie, his older sister, who was going to do his job for that time. Josh sputtered and disagreed with the punishment, but I stood firm.

* *

So a week after this event, on that fateful Friday, Zach and Stephanie were quick to get out of the door. Jerusha, who was only nine, took a little longer. She had to go up a hill with her little bike to get to her route, as our street ran down from an elevation on the South end of Barrie. About 4:00 pm the electricity went out and I was sure that it must be storming somewhere to have it go out as there was not a storm cloud to be seen in our area. I was helping Jerusha getting her papers together and she went out of the door. I do not recall how much time had gone by before noticing that the sky had turned a grey-green hue. It was an eerie color, and I felt an immediate danger. I ran out of the door, hoping to be able to call Jerusha back, standing in the middle of our street I saw her turn the corner on the top of Crawford onto Ardagh road. I used a finger whistle to call my children out of the bush for supper on many occasions, but this time the wind took the sharp sound my whistle eastward, never reaching Jerusha's ear. I called out to Joshua who was playing with the little ones, told him that we were in for quite a thunderstorm.

"Josh, you are to look after the children while I go to help Jerusha with her route" were my instructions. "Dad will be home soon!"

Feeling a little panicky and torn between leaving the little ones and rescuing Jerusha, I took the van and made it quickly to the road on the hill. As I was looking for Jerusha, I saw our neighbor boy, who was delivering a weekly newspaper. I called out to him to get in the van, told him of the imminent storm, took his little bike and put it in the back and continued checking the driveways for Jerusha. After I had them both safely in the van, I lost the knot in my stomach. No matter what, they were not going get soaked when the storm would come down, and the threat of a lightning strike was minimal once they were in the car.

We started at the end of the route, the children delivering the papers by running back and forth from the houses to the van. We were right across from Crawford Street when the storm unleashed its anger. Thunder and lightning were accompanied by torrential rains. The van was shaking, as the wind competed with the rain. It was short and immensely powerful. Not long after the skies cleared, and a bleak sun appeared in the west. The clouds that had moved to the east looked black and even more threatening with the sun shining on them. Nature seemed peaceful but only for a short while. When the children asked if they could resume delivering papers, I pointed up to the left behind me and said: "After **that** is gone!"

That was the tornado! Bits of papers and objects were flying around this cloud. Shayan, the little scientist, said that with the high winds, the hot and the cold air masses of that day, it could spur a tornado. I stated emphatically that no tornados would come to Barrie as we saw this dirty whirling cloud moving up the hill to the east of Barrie, rushing towards Allandale. I had never seen a tornado, not even in a movie, so I had nothing to compare with what I saw, to something that I knew. The tree that we were standing under lost quite a bit of branches but none of them targeted our van. We were thankful to be safe and dry. I had no idea of the destruction that had occurred just below us in the valley, and I encouraged the children to deliver the rest of the papers, as soon as the sun appeared again.

* *

As we were making our way to Essa Road, cars and big transport trucks were coming up on Ardagh Road. My thought was that a huge accident must have happened on the highway, so they all had to exit off to Essa Road. The traffic had come to a halt and people were out of their cars talking amongst one another. Someone came to my van and asked whether I had seen a young boy delivering newspapers.

"Yes, that boy is with me but is finishing his paper route at the moment," was my answer.

"His father is looking for him", was the reason for his question.

Then I saw Shayan's Dad coming towards the van, looking extremely worried.

"You have Shayan?"

After I calmed his fears, he made a little dance in the middle of the street, praising the Lord. I found it strange that he was looking for his son all the way up on Ardagh road. I told him that we would soon be home as they were almost done, and I would drop Shayan off at his house. He did not explain why he was concerned about where his son was or why he was so relieved that he was safe.

* *

I was to find that out on our way back home. We turned onto our street not expecting anything different. Lots of low trees and brush were on the left and the right side of our street, so you could not see the area on both sides of the street from the top of the hill. As we were going down Crawford Street a car stopped us, a young man commanded me to get the children away from the window:

"There are dead people out there!"

More surprised than anything else by the tone of his voice, I was trying to grasp what he had said, until we came to the part of the street that was not hedged by bushes and trees. Do not tell children 'not' to look, for they will do the opposite. They had their faces right close to the front and side window.

What came next was a view of utter destruction of my neighborhood. It looked like a bomb had hit the area. What was still standing was black from mud. Some houses had totally disappeared as others had still half of the structure standing with exposing the upstairs closet contents, clothes waving in the wind. Most trees were downed but some trees that were still standing had no bark left on the trunk and looked like white stick figures with branches like arms reaching up to the heavens in anguish. The bottom parts of some trees were covered with metal from cars and sheds and other items that were ripped from houses and backyards.

As a neighbor was being pulled from a pile of mud that was her home just minutes before, I called the children away from the window. She looked lifeless and the reality of what the young man had warned me about earlier, set in. Immediately I felt dread, what about my home and children. A series of thoughts rushed in, the house, the children, those at home and outside delivering papers? Then I saw the roof of our home above the cedars that lined our property.

"Thank you, Lord!"

But what about Stephanie who was delivering the papers? I was already nauseous because of the horrible sights, but now my throat was being squeezed. Zach's route was not in our neighbourhood, but still my hope was that he was not finished and therefore not close to our home yet.

I did not focus anymore on the carnage around me, but on what was coming up on the other side of the cedars. Our big silver maple that stood in the front yard was lying in front of the picture window with the root-system totally exposed. It was like a big hand scooped it out of the dirt and put it on its side.

As I stopped the van in front of the house, the children

including Stephanie were standing in what had been the front porch. They were crying and crying out to me:

"Come quick Mom, come quick!"

I must have been in shock as I did not dare step over the downed hydro wires, even though I knew before I went to find Jerusha, that the electricity was out. Stephanie encouraged me to get over them as a neighbour who came to check on the kids jumped over them. I did get my senses back and joined my little ones in front of the house.

Even though they looked upset, sad and bloodied, they were alive, what a relief! They stood in a sea of broken glass as we had the front porch enclosed with windows the year before. We went in the house and it did not look too bad in the front room, but the kitchen and living room were a disaster with branches, leaves and glass all over the place. Many tears were shed in that first hour. The children had found some cloths to bandage and bind up the cuts in the arms of 3 children. Stephanie had the worst injury as she was hit by a flying glass and debris standing right in front of that north window when it was shattered by branches. Her wrist was cut quite deep. I bandaged her wrist with some bandages cut into strips, to pull the big cut together. There were many pieces of glass in her hair, and I did not dare hugging her too tightly as the fine shards were all over her clothes. Once the children were looked after, we started to pick the pieces of glass and branches from the floor to make it safer for us to walk around. The big woolen carpet in the living room we just rolled up and put it outside. I took the shards of glass out of the window opening and put the window in that I had put on the floor after cleaning it. I only realized later what a special move that was, orchestrated by God. I had no understanding of my earlier action until later that night, when we were praising the Lord and thanking

Him for His protective hedge around our family. Yes, there was damage to our home and surroundings, but everyone in our family was alive and well even with some bandages.

* *

Stephanie told us her story. She had started her paper-route in a normal pace, but when the thunderstorm unleashed its fury, she ran like a hind, delivering newspapers that would never be read. She had started to collect from some neighbors but as soon as the thunderstorm hit the area and the rain soaked her thoroughly, she was going to leave it for the next day. As rain was coming down hard on her she wondered why no one asked her to come in and hide from the storm. Thankfully no one did and she made it home, soaked but safe. Samuel, my one-year-old was crying and she took him from Joshua. The phone rang and since I was not there to speak to our friend, Stephanie talked to her. After a minute or two she saw the cedars trees that lined the yard pushed all the way to down to the ground and the windows blew in. Joshua grabbed Samuel from her arm, ran to the bathroom taking the little ones with him. Stephanie turned to go there too but as she ran away from the blown-open window, she was still attached to the phone receiver. Her hand would not let go of the horn, she had to pry her fingers open with her free hand. She was in total shock. She then joined the children in the bathroom. That was absolutely the safest place in the house. It was situated in the middle, on the east side of the house. It must have been a terrifying couple of minutes for kids on their own, as the tornado swirled around the house with noise like a freight train in their ears.

* *

I had expected my husband to be home before the storm hit, but as he was on his way home with Arjan, the thunder, lightning and driving rain slowed them down to turtle speed. By the time they came to our neighborhood he was stopped by someone who asked him to take a gentleman to the hospital as he needed medical attention. He was bloody and muddy, and my husband realized it was our Dutch neighbor. He had no idea why this man was in such a state. Arjan walked home from that point and let us know why Dad was not home yet.

This neighbor's house was destroyed. Three people were in his home when the tornado hit. His wife's brother was visiting from the Netherlands and was brought to the hospital by another neighbor. Sadly, Mrs. Schooneveld was killed, her heart could not handle the shock of the impact that the tornado had on her home. She did not have fatal injuries, but a heart attack took her life.

Michael took Mr. S to the hospital and by the time he got there, there was no parking available because the injured came in droves to get help. He left the car in the driveway to the emergency department, left the keys in the ignition so once the car had to be moved it could be done without someone looking for the owner. He stayed with our neighbor for a while and cleaned him up a bit, until the nursing staff was able to look after him. Michael left the hospital and had a hard time finding his car. There were so many cars coming and going but had no idea why it was so busy. No one told him that a disaster had taken place. He did not find his car that day as someone had moved it, but a stranger drove him home. When he finally arrived home, I felt so relieved to see him healthy and well. The next day he went back to the hospital to retrieve his car.

*   *

Jerusha had 2 friends in our neighborhood her age, Nicki who lived just 3 houses up from ours and Paula who lived on Patterson Place. Many of the houses that were built on our street were for the Canadian servicemen that survived the 2nd World War. These were not built to withstand a F4 tornado. Nicki, her Mom, her little brother Danny and Paula were all in their home on the corner of Crawford Street and Patterson Place. The tornado wiped that little house off their property. The storm took the life of Nicki's Mom and little 5-year-old brother Danny. Paula also lost her life, and Nicki could not be found until much later. She was badly injured but was found in time to be taken to Sick Kids Hospital where she was taken care of for about 2 months.

Jerusha was a shy girl, and she lost her friend Paula in that terrible storm. Her friend Nicki was not around for a long time and for a 9-year-old that was a big adjustment to know it would never be the same. We thanked the Lord that Nicki got better physically, but I am sure it took a long time for her to adjust to life without her Mom and brother. Nicki and her Dad moved to BC later on and we had a chance to visit her there, which was quite emotional to say the least. She loves the Lord and will meet her Mom and brother in heaven.

*   *

Some points of consideration with thanksgiving.

Our house was damaged, but we were able to stay in our home while the repair to the house, which was quite extensive, was done over a period. We were told to go to the Armory in the middle of Barrie as the house according to the inspector was not structurally safe. We felt in our hearts to stay and camped, so to speak, in our home for the next couple of weeks until the electricity was restored, and water flowed once again from our well.

Because Joshua's wrongdoing he was not delivering the papers on this fateful day. Our son, who has a sweet disposition and was called a 'peach' by his kindergarten teacher, is not one to hurry and would have surely been taken from us, if he were out there delivering papers in the path of the tornado.

Stephanie was our cross-country runner and ran home as soon as the thunderstorm started and came in the house just before the tornado swirled around the neighborhood.

The windowpanes I had washed and put aside, closed the window opening on the North side, other windows we covered with plastic. We were protected from the outside for the next couple of weeks until new windows replaced the broken ones.

Benjamin who was 3 at the time, was sleeping on the couch in front of the big bay window in the living room and even though all the trees that the storm took down, laid with their roots facing west and the treetops east, the big Silver Maple in front of that window laid South to North parallel to the front of the house. The swing set that was standing just in front of that big window before the storm was found to the north of the house, a twisted mess. That bay window did not have one broken pane.

The thankfulness that was in our hearts for God's goodness and protection is indescribable. The realization of these amazing points of God's grace came only later. Little by little after the initial shock passed, we counted our blessings one by one.

"I will tell of the kindnesses of the Lord, the deeds for which he is to be praised, according to all the Lord has done for us—yes, the many good things he has done for Israel,

according to his compassion and many kindnesses." Isaiah 63:7

"Many, Lᴏʀᴅ my God, are the wonders you have done, the things you planned for us. None can compare with you; were I to speak and tell of your deeds, they would be too many to declare." Psalm 40:5

"Finally, brothers and sisters, whatever is true, whatever is noble, whatever is right, whatever is pure, whatever is lovely, whatever is admirable—if anything is excellent or praiseworthy—think about such things." Philippians 4:8

PART 3

PART 3

26

TEN IS ENOUGH

When our youngest child Emily was a year old, I weaned her. This was the norm that I had set for our children. Not always, but within a couple of months I would be pregnant again. The cult was losing its grip on us as we had distanced ourselves because of some questionable actions by the leaders.

* *

Michael came to me and told me that 10 children is enough. Even though I had turned my heart against many of the rules of the group about 3 years before this conversation, it came as a surprise and a bit of a shock. What was spoken to us through the years was that the Lord opens and closes the womb. That I never searched that out is on my own shoulders. I counted on the Lord to regulate the number of children we were to have because of that. So, when my husband made that statement, I was a little disturbed. To do the will of the Lord in every area of my life was my desire. Each baby was welcomed as a special gift of God. Every two years there was that special time of a new life that brought a wonderful atmosphere in our family. The next day I had some time to bring my concern to Jesus. I asked Him to give me peace.

"I want to please you Lord, but also honor my husband's decision."

The best thing to do was to search for a scripture or passage in His Word. After I prayed, I planned to just open my Bible up anywhere and trust that Jesus would guide me to what He wanted to tell me. As the Bible that I had in my hand was quite familiar, it was easy to open it either in the front or back and hope to read something I could hook into. I did not want any manipulation on my part, so I took my Bible and for the second time in my Christian walk, closed my eyes, turned the Bible every which way, opened it and put my finger on the page. It opened to the gospel of John 1. What could be there to give me peace about my concern?

Starting at John 1:9 I read: 9 *The true light that gives light to everyone was coming into the world. 10 He was in the world, and though the world was made through him, the world did not recognize him. 11 He came to that which was his own, but his own did not receive him. 12 Yet to all who did receive him, to those who believed in his name, he gave the right to become the children of God-- 13* **children born not of natural descent, nor of human decision or a husband's will, but born of God**

John 1:9-13

* *

My eyes stuck to the last part and realized that the Lord does not control our will in any way shape or form. His desire for those that are born is to become the children of God, to be born-again! He even allows us to decide the number of children we like to have. Certainly, there could be a medical condition to sway our plans, but He leaves us free. He gives us guidelines and commands, but it is still up to us to follow His bidding.

I felt free and relieved! Since my eyes were opened to this truth, I searched for the 'scripture' that had been our guide in this area for the last 10 years. "God opened her womb" was about the women that were infertile, and the Lord gave them a child. There is a scripture that tells us that the Lord enabled Rachel to conceive.

"Then God remembered Rachel; he listened to her and enabled her to conceive." Gen.30:22

Nothing there about closing a womb!

Shall I bring to the time of birth, and not cause delivery?" says the Lord. *"Shall I who cause delivery shut up the womb?" says your God.* Isaiah 66:9 NKJV

* *

Amazed at myself that I had not searched this out when we joined the 'Fellowship'. But the Lord meant for the 5 younger ones to be here, for which I am so thankful and could not imagine a life without them. He was there through it all and has a call on each of them.

We are thankful for the children we have, proud of the adults they have become and grateful for each grandchild that they have given us.

27

WATER IN THE BOAT

The analogy of a marriage being like a boat on the sea of life is age old. Just like a sailor on a ship, one will experience calm waters and turbulent seas. Is one prepared for the first storm? Not likely! As you 'stay' on that ship, in time you will learn to deal with every kind of weather and situations that come with sailing a ship, major or minor problems. Trying to circumvent storms does not often work as they sometimes come as a surprise. So, you go through the storm and pray the boat will stay afloat.

* *

As we married just 2 days before we immigrated to Canada, we entered into the unknown as a couple. I loved my husband for his tenderness, and great humour. We had a great time on the ship that sailed us to our new destination. Someone had robbed us of the money that was gifted to us on our wedding day, but that did not dampen our spirits. It concerned us but since we were going to my aunt in Toronto, it did not worry us too much.

* *

Our first test came while we were waiting for the train in Montreal. No money to buy lunch or dinner, we became cranky. Without proper nutrition for 15 hours and now feeling the pinch of 'poverty', there was a good number of irritable words towards each other. Once in the train at 6 pm and the knowledge that we would not arrive until midnight, we snuggled and snoozed for these couple of hours of travel.

* *

We did well until Michael took a second job at a nursing home in the kitchen, when we lived in Thornhill. He was a good-looking guy, athletic and a smart dresser. At one point he did not come home on his usual time, and I demanded that he tell me why he was so late. We had our first fight! I was feeling that he did not give me the attention a husband should and was jealous! Of what? I really could not put my finger on anything specific, but my heart was in pain. That was not really a storm that made our boat rock, just a good wind that was testing the strength of the walls and bottom of the boat. The problem was solved and soon we entered again into calmer waters.

* *

In 1968 we were anticipating the birth of our first child. That was an exciting time. Our ship was sailing with full sails. We were happy. Financially it was a bit of a struggle when I was not working the first couple of months after our son's birth. But when Zach was about 2 months old, a telephone call came from the hospital where I worked as a lab technician to please come back as soon as I felt able. Once again, we were making it from paycheck to paycheck, and paid our bills on time. Thankfully, we were mostly on the same page when it came to making decisions and rolled with the punches.

* *

When we got born-again in 1972, I grew in faith through the reading of His word, I was thankful for what He had already given to us: a family. We had two growing boys and a little girl. I learned how to trust Him through different situations, and through reading the real-life stories of believers that stood the test of faith in some very harsh conditions. On hearing of a certain couple that had a marriage break-up, I thanked God that as I was His follower, He would not allow that to happen to me!! That was not a word from the Lord, but I believed that something like a break-up would never happen to one that loves the Lord. He had other plans, plans of testing and trial. I am sure 'He' knew that I could stand the test. When these trials come upon us it often shows 'us' what is in our hearts. Faith, hope, and love are truly the 3 foundations that can be shaken in severe testing.

* *

When something happened at the 'Fellowship' that was blatantly opposite of the teaching of the scriptures I was done with it all. For me, the pail of controversies was full and overflowing. Michael and I discussed a way to break away the group. We had the bakery to consider as many of the employees were connected to the fellowship and some had large families. They had also followed the teaching, that the Lord opens and closes the womb. The following couple of days I prayed for a way to tell them that I was not coming back. The leader phoned me later in that week and used some scriptures to sway my decision. Why I allowed this man to smooth talk me in staying, I have no answer for, but I made an exit from it all in my heart. About 4 families left the 'Fellowship'. An adulterous and lying spirit entered the group. We as a family stayed, but my heart was not there anymore.

*   *

My husband grew distant, and I suspected that he had turned his eyes away from his family. I was not the most important person in his life anymore. Some things that he would say to me were like a foreign language as he had never used offensive words to me before. I was experiencing heartache, but in time I got to know what it felt like to have it shredded. Every Sunday morning, we would get up late and prepare breakfast for our large family. Some days it would be bacon and eggs, other times pancakes and sometimes Michael would make scrumptious English muffins. After our brunch we get ready to be at the meeting at 2 pm. Before my suspicions hung in the air, I enjoyed our relaxing Sunday mornings, but the tension at breakfast time must have been felt by the children. One of these Sundays, I was standing at the counter and Michael close to me at the stove. I had my housecoat on, and Michael had his dress pants on but was still in his pyjama top. Regular relaxed conversation between the two of us was not the norm anymore. Emily, who was not quite 2 yet came between the two of us and got a hold of my housecoat and grabbed her Daddy's pyjama top and put them together. I was overtaken with emotion but did not want anyone to notice. I whisked away the tears and carried on with the preparation of the meal. I felt it was a sign of the Lord that it was going to be OK. I was a little naïve in the belief that 'the OK' would be just around the corner.

*   *

Early that following year, a friend who was vacationing for 2 weeks in Jamaica called us. The friend that she was traveling with had to return home because of an emergency and asked if our two oldest boys would be able to join her for the last week of her stay. Both Michael and I did not think it was a wise thing to send them there. It was in the middle of the 2nd term of school, and it would cost twice the fare to fly them there. My husband encouraged me to go. I was quite surprised for him to let me go on a vacation. He said it would be good for me to have a holiday. Looking back a couple of years later I realized that he felt the freedom to step over the line and break his marriage vows. I was in the dark and wanted to believe that a relationship with the Lord was most important in his live too. And of course, something like 'that' would not happen to me, as I loved the Lord so much!

*   *

In the early summer of 1989, we had purchased a Restaurant in Midhurst. We had left 'the Fellowship' and were looking forward to a 'normal' Christian life with our family. We also made plans to go to the Netherlands as my Mom and Dad had an Anniversary party planned in September. It would be their 45th year of married life. It was an exciting time for the children and me. I threw myself in the preparations for this event. The children had saved up money from their paper routes and we increased the mortgage to have enough to buy the restaurant and vacation for a couple of weeks in the Netherlands.

It was a wonderful time there. It was the first time in my parents' life to have all their grandchildren in one place and to see them interact with their cousins was a highlight in their life. It also put my husband in a different setting, and we had a great time together. I just wanted to stay in Holland as the interaction between Michael and I was great.

* *

Once we were back at home, clouds were once again gathering and the winds gaining strength over the next couple of months. A dear sister-in-the-Lord who was also my confidante and dear friend, invited me for a coffee as she did not want to meet in our home but a restaurant. She felt that I should know the truth as she heard that my husband was having an affair. I was in shock and wanted to confront him right away. She advised against it and told me to war in the spirit. I found that hard to do as I was angry and hurt. I had wanted to war with my fists rather than in my spirit. The day after, I was mostly on my knees weeping and praying as I felt He let me down and did not protect me the way that 'I' felt that He should have.

* *

I did not want to speak to my husband about my knowledge of his transgression in anger but wanted to know what was in his heart about the future of his family. What about the children? I did not get any definite answers. I am sure he was torn and not at peace with the situation as he loved his children dearly.

The Lord laid it on my heart to work in the restaurant from opening to closing. Also, as I was before God in prayer, He pressed it upon my heart to fast. I did not have breakfast or lunch but had a small supper, as I did not want my children or Michael to know that I was fasting. In this time, I was starting to have total faith that the Lord was going to restore our relationship and make it better than it was before. We had left 'the Fellowship' physically behind us but now 'the Fellowship' had to get out of us. We went to a Pentecostal church and the pastor helped us financially to get marriage counselling. There we had a chance to talk about our grievances toward each other and get some solid advice. I was still fasting, and it had been many months since I started and asked the Lord how much longer as I had lost a lot of weight. He spoke to my heart: Soon!

* *

When we purchased the restaurant, the realtors Sylvia Szynech and her husband had a contest going for anyone who used their services to buy or sell property in that year. The contest closed before December 1989. On the 10th of that month, we got a visit from this couple. We were standing in the kitchen area of the restaurant and received the news that we had won the trip to St Lucia. What a wonderful gift! I was excited, but Michael was quite cool; I understood his reaction. In time we both got to know that the Lord was in this and He used this couple and the gift of the trip to start the repair of our relationship.

* *

I can write about this period in our marriage on a couple of pages, but it took following the tips that our counsellor offered and many more years of trusting the Lord for healing of broken trust and frayed emotions. The trip to St Lucia was a much-needed break away from the everyday cares and we were able to talk openly about what happened and find forgiveness for each other's shortcomings.

Truly, love conquers all. In time we joined the Vineyard

in Barrie and under the wonderful ministry of Pastor Peter Jackson, Michael found deliverance, freedom and healing; and I received healing and comfort through the love of Heather, the pastor's wife.

* *

On our 45th Anniversary Michael surprised me. It was almost Easter and the snow was gone, but in our area the weather could turn on a dime and become winterlike until the half of May. It had become a tradition for Michael and me to treat the children and grandchildren to a Dutch breakfast. We tried to do the same as my Mom's breakfasts, she provided for Easter celebrations so many years ago. Since it was often an early Easter and the chance for snow, hail and sleet was great, Micheal would plan the egg hunt according to the weather conditions. One year he made a labyrinth not formed by high hedges but snowy walls. It was great fun for the grands to have a totally different egg hunt that particular year. Sometimes it would be a late Easter and the chocolate eggs were melting in the warm sun. Then it was a treat to have the breakfast outside.

* *

Even though Easter was later in April 2011, the weather forecast was unsettling. He had started to set up the party tents we had purchased a couple of years before, to have our family gatherings in reasonable comfort. I thought it was a bit early as it was still 10 days before Easter, but since he did it all on his own, I understood that he wanted it in place in good time.

My daughters invited me for breakfast the Sunday before Easter. I thoroughly enjoy the company of my girls, but breakfast was not the only thing they treated me to. Afterwards they took me shopping. Dress, shoes and jewelry were on that menu. I was totally surprised at the beautiful things they bought me. Then they took me to a house close to us for me to get dressed in my new outfit and do my hair and make-up. By that time I had the feeling that pictures would be taken because of the Anniversary that was just the Wednesday before. My oldest daughter had a friend in our neighborhood that was a photographer and worked from her home. But as they were driving me and turned into our street I was quite confused. Maybe they were going home to pick up my husband?

We entered the house and my oldest son greeted me with a big bouquet of flowers and guided me through the hall to the backyard. There my husband was standing at the entrance of the tents with a ring and asked me to marry him all over again. Tears flowed from his and my eyes and we walked together towards the front where our Pastor friend stood to perform the ceremony. He had to come from quite a distance north from us and drove through a snowstorm to bless us. Family and close friends were there to witness to outflow of the miracle that the Lord performed some 20 years before.

Today we are in our golden years and in God we have experienced SO MANY beautiful moments. We will celebrate 55 years together in 2021.

28

EMPATHY

After we were free from the cult, we joined the Pentecostal church in our city. It took some time before we stepped over the fear that had held us for such a long time.

Fear that if I would wear something black, I was out of favour with God. Fear that if I trimmed a bit of my hair, the anointing would be cut.

Fear that if we would go to a doctor, the Lord would not give us health. This kind of fear was truly created by indoctrination of a God that had a big hammer and if one would sidestep, there was no mercy. Little by little this would disappear in the background, as we learned again about the amazing grace of God. I think we went for prayer every time an altar call was given. Freedom was apparent for me when I dared to buy a pair of black pants and had my hair shortened to shoulder length.

* *

When I was a child, I was fearless in many activities that were undertaken by my peers. We would be playing leapfrog and jumped over one that stood just with their head bent and some would, including me, clear that jump without a problem. We never gave a thought to the chance we might end up with a face plant on the sidewalk.

Another favorite was pole jumping over the ditches that were full of water. We choose the ones that were full to the top and just like pole vaulting, take a run, stick the pole in the middle, and go over the ditch. Of course, the challenge was not to get wet. It occurred a few times that my pole would stick in the middle and sink in the mud. I had no choice but to slide down that pole and end up in the dirty water as the previous jumpers had stirred up quite some sludge. The foul smell was another reason you needed to get clear over the ditch. Once home I would get a good punishment. Mom had enough to do without cleaning a child that had been warned not to do such things.

As a teenager we sometimes had to ride a bike over a road that was approximately a kilometer long and had no streetlights. Stories were going around that you had to be careful about men that would attack you, if you dared to bike there. They might have been just stories to scare you, as kids around that age love to do to others. I told them that I had no problem riding my bike or even walking on that road in the dark or otherwise. It was not in me to be fearful of things that in my mind I could control. I was strong, had taken some Ju-Jitsu classes, not any higher than a yellow belt, but it made me confident that I could face a challenge and win. Thank God I was never tested in that area. As an adult I was interested in the unknown and sought out the occult sphere. Curious more than anything, I had no fear as I had no idea that there would be repercussions. Even then, as I told in my story earlier, I felt guilty and ashamed of the thoughts that entered my mind, but not a constant feeling of suffocating fear.

* *

I also wanted to go skydiving, ballooning and ziplining. These kinds of activities I dreamt about in my younger years. Not until I was retired, that we were given the opportunity to go canyoning, white water rafting and ziplining. Today there is no longer the push anymore for me to try out new and exciting things.

Before Jesus Christ became my Lord and Saviour, I could not understand that one could have a phobia. Secretly I judged those that spoke about fearing something, either real or imagined. But God has ways to teach His children humbleness, and an attitude of consideration and compassion.

* *

Our family often went camping and took daytrips together. One spot we visited more than once in our area is called "The Big Chute Marine Railway". It is part of the Trent-Severn Waterway. It connects Lake Ontario with Lake Huron. You can navigate your boat through 368 km of canals but must go through quite a few locks as Lake Huron at Georgian Bay is approximately 334 feet higher than Lake Ontario at the Bay of Quinte. There are 45 locks in the system. It took 70 years to complete this enormous undertaking. It could have been completed a lot sooner, but politics and corruption were the cause for the delay of the finished project.

* *

Today it is a beautiful trip for boaters to spend a vacation or retirement on the water and go from north to south or the other way around. One of the locks is at Port Severn. This particular lock is not controlled by the leveling out the water but lifts the boats out of the water on a carriage riding on a set of rails, over a hill that has a road running right over it, hence the name Marine Railway.

The upper part of the lake connects with the lower part with a beautiful waterfall that does not have an instant drop but goes through a narrow passage of rocks and boulders. It has a 60-foot drop and is called the Little Chute. It is very picturesque with its cascading water.

* *

When we visited that area, our children would jump into the water just past the rocks and were carried by that 'white' water to the last part of the river where it opened into the lower lake. They swam to the shore to do it all over again.

It was great for them to see the engineering feat of the boats being cradled in a carriage that would take them up and over the road into the upper or lower lake, but the kids were more interested in the fast water. We would spend a whole day there with a picnic lunch.

* *

When our youngest was about 4 we revisited the Chute. What a change from the one that we saw a couple of years before. This time there was a warning sign at the Little Chute. No swimming allowed! That was such a disappointment for our kids. The area where the boats came over the road had nice sidewalks now and there was a high cement wall that divided the Little from the Big Chute. The top of the cement structure was about a foot wide on the top. I had no idea if there was a restriction to walk on that wall, but the 2 older ones and my husband started to go across it. Michael had Emily in front of him by the hand, 6 in front of me, with Benjamin behind me. Almost halfway the wall, I was gripped by anxiety about being up high and feared I would fall. I could not move, felt kind of dizzy and weak in the knees. My pounding heart and nauseous feeling made it only worse. I called out to my husband:

"I can't go on!"

"What? Why?"

"I am going to fall" I must have squeaked it out.

"Well, you can't go back, so just put one foot in front of the other" was his answer to my panic.

"I can't!"

Everyone had stopped walking by now and some looked back. Now I even feared for the ones that did not have their eyes on the wall in front of them. I do not know how long we paused, but Benjamin behind me said:

"Mom, give me your hand".

I dared to move my arm ever so slowly behind me and Benjamin took my hand. After a minute or so he said:

"Mom, I prayed for you, you can walk now".

Amazing how peace came over me and even though my heart was still beating fast, the dizziness left and with his hand in mine I took a step. It became easier as I kept 'putting one foot in front of the other' as my husband had instructed me. We all made it safely to the end of the wall.

*   *

Today this wall has barbed wire on top of a 6-foot-high chain link fence. Signs are posted in strategic areas warning of the danger of fast flowing water. They were not there 30 years ago.

I never had an episode of panic or anxiety after that, but it certainly changed my heart towards those that have these crippling experiences. It makes me strong in battling for them, as I do believe they are an attack of Satan.

29

OH, MY PAPA

My Dad was born on 19-01-1919 into a family that counted 16 children in total. Even though this family went through World War I and II, they were not severely affected financially by the poor economy of these unfortunate upheavals. They were resourceful and hard workers.

When Dad and Mom married at the end of World War II, they had to walk to church as there was nothing left by that time in the area of convenience in all aspects of life. But both were intent on making a happy life together even in this difficult time of war and uncertainty. The year after, they had a little daughter and in the ensuing years their family grew to 7 children.

Dad was very happy when a little boy was born. Of course, his name had to be Peter. I have a picture of a great-grandfather, grandfather or *Opa*, my Dad and my baby brother. All with the name Peter Pouw.

* *

As a child I accompanied my Dad often to the large vegetable garden that was feeding his growing family.

Vegetables and potatoes were the main meal of the day, which was totally provided for through his efforts, and for the protein portion, a milk product as dessert. We did get meat, but only on Sundays and fish on Fridays as a good Catholic family should. Father was an excellent provider and there was not a day that we went hungry or lacked the necessities of life. After we emigrated, I received letters from my Mom, but when I received a letter from my Dad I was over the moon.

Mom came to visit us quite often, but Dad was not so keen to travel by air. Finally, Mom got him so far that he agreed to spend his vacation time with our family.

* *

It was in 1972 that my Dad made his first visit to Canada. At that time, we lived in Downsview. Stephanie was 3 months old, Zach just turned 4 in November and Arjan was going on 3 early in the year to come. He enjoyed his grandchildren more than anything else. Dad loved exploring Toronto on his own; he took the bus to go downtown and did not return until supper time. I think I have some of those genes as I love to drive and find new roads to reach to a certain destination.

Dad's visit was about one year after that we had committed our lives to the Lord. We shared with him all we had learned about relationship with God instead of religion. We told him about our experience of water baptism in the Credit River and tackled the Catholic belief of Purgatory. Some of our discussions were a bit heated but thankfully Dad accepted the Bible as the Word of God and we were able to go to the scriptures to see what God had to say about some of his or our beliefs. We could not sway him;

as in his mind we had fallen away from the true church, but we loved and honored him. I was quite zealous but had to learn to 'let go and let God'.

* *

It was not until my father's last days on earth that I learned how these conversations had impacted his spiritual life.

My Dad was diagnosed with bone cancer when he was in his mid-sixties. He was in pain all the time as bone cancer, sickness of Kahler or multiple myeloma made the whole skeletal system ache. Still, he and Mom came to Canada for a holiday when our youngest child, Emily was about 6 months old. They even made the trip to Nova Scotia with us to meet up with their old friends, who emigrated to Canada around 1954. It was the highlight of their vacation. Except for many naps through the day, my father did not show any signs of slowing down. Over the next years the illness progressed, but still he made the trip in 1992 to be part of a wedding of our oldest son Zach. A year and a half later he became to sick to enjoy the simple things of life. His kidneys were not functioning anymore, and all other vital organs were failing.

* *

One Saturday morning in the end of August 1993, I was called by my sister Marianne from the Netherlands:

"If you do not come quickly, you will not see Papa alive as he is dying and already unconscious".

That was not an unexpected message as Dad was diagnosed with his disease six years prior to her call. Still when the time came for him to exit this present world, it still was a shock for the near and dear ones.

The desire to be there was great; but the finances to pay for this unexpected trip were not so great. While I was discussing the probability of traveling and possibility of paying for the flight to the Netherlands, we had a knock on the door. My father's oldest sister Polly and her daughter decided to come for coffee that morning. My cousin had regular contact with me, but the only time I would see my aunt was when we would go to her home in Cambridge, Ontario.

She was 11 years older than my Dad and was the big sister that took care of the little baby boy that was named after his father Piet. There they were, standing in my kitchen just after I had received the news of my Dad's serious condition.

"*Tante* Polly, Papa is dying" I said choking back the tears.

"Oh, mijn *kleine Pietje*": Oh, my little Piet, she said.

She held me and sternly said: "You are going to see him, yes?"

"I would love to go, but we have no money for the flight" was my answer.

Even before we had our coffee, she wrote me a blank cheque for a trip to see my Dad for the last time. I was intensely thankful for God's provision and blessed my aunt for her generosity.

After lunch I was going to go to a travel agency to see if there were any flights available that evening or the next day. With a shock I realized that it was Saturday and in 1993 most, if not all, travel agencies were closed.

Still I took the telephone book and searched for an agency that was open for business. Then I remembered that Sears had a travel agency, and they were always open on a

Saturday but did not know if they were open all afternoon. With my heart beating in my throat, I drove to that store in record time. The lady across the desk was kind as I shared with tears in my eyes, that my father was dying, and I needed to get a trip as soon as possible to the Netherlands. She said that I could get a compassionate flight but had to show a death certificate on my return. The first flight out was not until Sunday evening, around 11 pm. That meant I would arrive in Amsterdam around noon on Monday. Still it would be almost 2 full days before I could be by his side. Constant prayer went up to God for Dad to still be there when I would arrive at the hospital. A thought came to me, while praying. 'Phone the hospital'.

I called my sister Marianne to tell her of the time I would be arriving on the Monday and that I would be staying for a week and asked if she had the number to the hospital.

"He is unconscious, and it is midnight" she replied.

"Yes, I realize that, but I really feel I have to call".

As soon as I ended the conversation with my sister, I called the hospital in which Dad was being treated. The nurse that answered on his floor was not very willing to put the phone to my Dad's ear.

"I am calling from Canada and would appreciate if you would do that" I pleaded.

"Ma'am, he is unconscious, there is no use", she said.

After I made some conversation with her, she agreed to put the horn to my Dad's ear.

"Dad, *Cokkie* here from Canada, I will be coming to Holland to see you and will be in your room on Monday around noon. You are not allowed to leave us yet OK?"

I strongly believe that, even though one is unconscious, their spirit senses what is going on around them.

After I hung up, I prayed again for God to keep my Dad

alive until I could be there with my family to see him for the last time on this side of the gulf that is fixed between us and eternity.

* *

The flight to Amsterdam was an uneventful 6 hours. My sisters were there to welcome me and take me to the hospital. I felt a bit uneasy, as I did not know what my Dad would look like at this stage of the disease. To my surprise my father was conscious when we entered his room. It was a tearful encounter, with gentle hugs as his body was in great pain.

As the family members could not stay with Dad because of them having to care for their children or work, I had nothing better to do than to stay with my father. A cot was provided for me to spend the nights beside Dad. Every other day I went home with my sister to get showered and change my clothes.

It was a peaceful couple of days with some conversation when Dad felt the need to tell me things that he had on his heart. He told me that he had spoken with my sister Josje about losing the battle with cancer and that he was too tired to go on. Josje had breast cancer, diagnosed when she was only 34 years of age. She had an operation and the necessary treatment to stop this terrible disease. He also said that even though they had promised each other to battle together, he had no more strength to continue the fight. Josje had become quite upset about that, understandably so.

In the short conversations that we had in those last days, he said that if I would not have been able to be at his side before his death, that Josje was to tell me that he was going to that place that we had spoken about together and that it was not Purgatory! He was going to make heaven his home!

That statement brought me back to 1972, when he was visiting Canada for the first time and we searched the scriptures together for the truth about this dogma. Even though at that time he did not agree with what I had to say about this belief, he must have changed his mind later.

A Catholic would have had the last rites administered when death was imminent, but he just wanted communion with my Mom.

* *

About halfway through that week, he conveyed his desire to die at home. Mother was not at all in favour of this. She said that she could not handle having Dad at home in his last days. I understood her objections as she was herself not in the best of health, mentally as well as physically.

"Mom, I am with you, I will not be visiting anyone else, but look after you and Dad" I told her.

She agreed and the wheels were set in motion to get this very sick patient back to his own home. It took a couple of days for it to become a reality. A hospital bed had to be put in the bedroom of their seniors' home and nursing staff was organized to assist in Dad's care.

He was brought back home on a Monday, a week after my arrival. Who would have known that Dad was not leaving us yet as his organs were already shutting down before I had even planned this trip!

Since the trip to Holland was only for a week, I was in contact with the airline to lengthen my stay. The KLM agent told me that it was possible to get an extension. Most likely I had to pay extra and show a death certificate at the airport when I was ready to return home. I had no extra money with me but left that in the capable hands of God.

Every year in the beginning of September there was a fair in our little village. It was held at the time of Dad's return home. Even the marching band would have its trip through the streets of our town.

My *Opa* was responsible for starting this band in our village. My Dad and his brother were members; one played the tuba and Dad the English horn. Tuesday was the time for the band to march. The band leader knew that my father had returned home and had a wonderful surprise in store for him. I do not know if the band had already chosen their marching route for that year, but they made their way to my parent's house. We opened the front and bedroom doors as they played especially for Dad. He was weeping as the music filled the room. Those that were present for this beautiful tribute were all in tears.

By that evening I knew that it was not long before Dad would breathe his last.

The call went out early that Wednesday morning to my siblings.

"Make your way to your father's side and hurry".

A nurse came to wash Dad and the doctor gave him an injection with a narcotic as he was crying out in pain when they put on a clean pyjama. After that he was lying very still and did not communicate anymore.

It was a little after lunch time that our father crossed over into eternity. Mom and all his children were at his side.

To be absent from the body is to be present with the Lord: II Cor. 5:8.

I knew that he was joining the angels in praise and joy the moment he left this earth to be in the presence of his Savior.

* *

The next couple of days were filled with planning the funeral. It was a wonderful thing that I could be part of that with my sisters and brother.

There were also other things to be thinking of before I could fly back home as I had to obtain the death certificate in another town and phone the airline to make sure there was a seat available. They could not tell me at that time or how much extra I had to pay. It was weighing heavily on me as we did not have any extras in the financial area.

When I was a teenager I would go to my aunt after high school. She lived on a road that I cycled going home. I would get a cup of tea and we would have lots of laughs and I would tell lots of stories about anything that would enter my mind. Her son was her only child and lost his Mom to cancer a couple of years prior to my Dad's passing.

My cousin heard about my missed flight and that it would cost some money to get back to my family. He came over to my parent's house before the funeral and handed me some money.

He said, "So you can go back to Canada even if you have to stay for another week".

I did not count out how much he gave but thanked him and gave him a big hug. Later that night I counted out what the gift amounted to: 2000 guilders! I could not believe my eyes and counted again. I had never held that amount of money in my hand before and thanked the Lord for this generous young man. No more worries even if the flight home would cost me as much as the return ticket. It was all taken care of, Jehovah Jirah, my provider. He uses whomever He chooses for His children to be looked after.

I felt so blessed! Later at the funeral I thanked my cousn again and told him how much I appreciated his kindness.

* *

It was time for me to say goodbye to my family after two emotional weeks.

I presented the death certificate to the agent at the check-in counter. She had to consult with her superiors on how much I was to pay to fly back. I always find myself a bit anxious at airports, and butterflies do not leave my stomach until I am seated in the plane. This time I felt at peace even though it took some time before she came back.

"Mrs. M there is no extra charge. It is part of the compassionate flights that are available to those that need them."

Tears welled up in my eyes as I was staring at her in unbelief. Such monetary gifts within one week were quite overwhelming. I was so thankful.

Once I was home again, surrounded by my husband and children the grieving process started, for which I had no time after my father died.

The place for me to let it all go was while I was by myself driving the car down the highway. I was thinking back on some special moments and treasuring the time that I was able to spend with Dad in the large vegetable garden; the bike trips that my siblings and I made with him through the Dutch countryside and the vacations that he spent with our family in Canada.

I know that I shall meet him again when I shall pass over into a blessed eternity.

30

MIGRAINES

Since I was about 10 years old I started to have migraine headaches.

According to the medical professionals head injuries are a cause, but stress and certain foods are likely culprits.

On occasion I took care of my neighbor's baby. In those days it was quite normal to babysit when 9 or 10 years old. It was a sunny day and my neighbour called upon me for help as she had so much housework. I was encouraged to take the little one to the playground which was about a 3-minute walk from our home. I did not have a baby carriage as usually a pram was available to keep a baby safe. So I carried that little one there and rocked her on the swing. I did not have my arms around the cords that held the swing but just sat on the seat holding the baby on my lap. Some boys were playing tag and ran around the swing set. I did not see danger, otherwise I would have taken a different position in holding the baby. One of the boys ran past me and pulled on the cord to my left which made me lose my balance. I held on tight to the little one and fell backwards on the ground. In those days they did not have sand as a cover but a cement pad. I hid my head on the pavement, and immediately saw stars and felt nauseous. I got up and walked home as fast as I could. I struggled to keep the baby in my arms and see the street in front of me. As I dropped the baby off at my neighbours and she asked if I wanted some lunch. It was the last thing that I wanted to think about as by now my stomach was not willing to hold what it contained. I shook my head and quickly went home. I was glad I reached the sink in the kitchen to be sick to my stomach. Mom wanted to know what happened, and I must have been able to tell her. I had an excruciating headache. She tucked me in bed and made the room dark. She called the doctor which was no easy feat in those days. If anyone wanted to call someone, they had to phone from a neighbour that had a business. I do not remember much of those days in bed, but one thing stood out. My Mom called my name, it sounded like it came from a great distance and I tried to answer but could not. The doctor came and told Mom to keep me in the dark for 10 days, staying flat on my back. Eventually the fog in my head disappeared, and much later in my life linked the injury to my head, to the start of frequently returning headaches. It might not have been completely from an injury as many of my family members suffered from migraines, but it sure did not help.

* *

Once I had a job, I had to take days off as I would be sick to my stomach because of the migraines. This would continue throughout my life. I would take pain medication in order to just function and to be able to take care of my children. When we attended 'The Fellowship', I did not take any and I just suffered for up to 3 days before the migraine would dissipate. Many times they would tip-toe around me while I was on the couch in a darkened living room.

Throughout my Christian walk, I had prayer such as instructed in James 5:13-16

Is anyone among you in trouble? Let them pray. Is anyone happy? Let them sing songs of praise. ¹⁴Is anyone among you sick? Let them call the elders of the church to pray over them and anoint them with oil in the name of the LORD. ¹⁵And the prayer offered in faith will make the sick person well; the LORD will raise them up. If they have sinned, they will be forgiven. ¹⁶Therefore confess your sins to each other and pray for each other so that you may be healed. The prayer of a righteous person is powerful and effective.

After we had come out of the cult I sought help from the medical profession again, hoping that something new was on the market to help me. There were no new treatments and resigned to the fact that there was nothing available that would alleviate the headaches. Sometimes the vomiting would not stop, and I end up in emergency department and they would get some fluids into me intra-venously. There was no cure! My prayers for healing never stopped! I knew Jesus was my only hope for healing in this area.

* *

We attended 'Jubilee Celebration Centre' when I was in my late sixties. In 2014 our pastor had invited an evangelist from Australia to come to our church in Orillia. We always looked forward to these events with special speakers and it was usually for a whole weekend. It was the Sunday night service, and I loved the worship joining in with all my heart. But soon I could not see the words of the song on the overhead projector screen. An aura took my vision away. Squiggly, moving patterns that flashed lights from the inner to the outer eye. I knew it was the precursor to another migraine. I said within myself: *"Oh no Lord, please not now."* After the worship I went out into the hall and took some pain medication with codeine, which was the only thing that gave me some relief and thus a chance to be able to listen to our visiting speaker. The drummer of the band was taking a drink and came to me.

"You are not looking good Corine" he said.

"Another migraine" was my short but all telling answer.

The young man held me around my shoulder and prayed for healing. I went back into auditorium and joined my husband, and hoped I would not get sick to my stomach. After the evangelist's message he turned to his left and asked if there was someone with a migraine headache. I was sitting in that section of the room and put my hand up immediately. Then he asked if there were others who suffered with these headache. Maybe they did not have one at that time, but called out those that are prone to migraines. About nine people stood up and he prayed a general prayer over us that had this debilitating medical problem. He also asked what the triggers were, and there were at least 5 different reasons for the start of these headaches. Never before in such meetings that I attended I heard a call out for healing from migraines, and I knew that this was the time for me to find relief from this bane. After the prayer the pain went away completely! I was thanking Jesus over and over again. On our way home, which was about a half an hour drive, I got another aura in my eye. I rebuked the enemy of our health and said:

"I am healed!"

By the time we came home the aura had disappeared

and I rejoiced as there was no headache after. I woke up in the middle of the night and again there was an aura. Again I claimed victory over this by thanking Jesus for my healing and reminding myself that a 'Word of Knowledge' was spoken over me and that could have only come from God. That was the end of this life-long struggle with migraines. No more blinding headaches! No more being sick to my stomach because of the pain!! Glory Hallelujah!!

In September of that special year we had a Caribbean cruise booked and my brother Peter and his wife were going to join us. We travelled by car to Miami and had a motel room close to the harbour. Early in the morning we had to get our suitcases ready and be in line to get a taxi to where the ship was docked. The hall of the motel room was filled with those that were waiting for a taxi to get them to their destination. It seemed that they were all going on this particular cruise. There was a lot of bumping into each other. We felt rushed and the wait for a taxi was a bit unnerving to say the least. Once we arrived at the site where our ship was moored, we were instructed to leave our suitcases standing in the middle of the parking area among multiple other suitcases and continue without them to the ship. My brother did not look too well and said:

"I'm getting a headache!"

He also suffered with migraines throughout his life.

"NOT ME!" I exclaimed.

This was truly the biggest test and a confirmation of the healing that took place a couple of months earlier. What a faithful God we serve. Never give up hoping and believing for healing or deliverance from a medical condition. His timing is perfect even if it takes its time. For me it took 43 years from the time I was saved, but God is never late. He knows what we need.

Patience, to accept delay without being angry or frustrated, He sure knows that we all need help with that. Perseverance and determination are necessary attributes in our Christian walk.

Matthew 7:7 *Ask and keep on asking, and it shall be given to you. Seek and keep on seeking, and you shall find. Knock and keep on knocking, and the door shall be opened unto you.*

IN CLOSING

Writing these stories made me relive the miracles that Jesus performed in our family. He will always be our hope and stay and when we are singing the song about the faithfulness of God in our life, both my husband and I choke up each time we sing it.

Michael had prostate cancer a couple of years ago, and as we were leaving the doctor's office after the news, it was God who impressed upon us both to have it removed rather than going through laser therapy. Yes, it is invasive, and the immediate aftereffects are not pleasant, but we obeyed. Michael did not need any chemo and has been cancer free since the operation. He has shown His grace through many healings as our bodies grow older.

We as a couple still make mistakes and not always hear or are not sensitive to the still voice of our Saviour and then we reap the fruit of our doing, which is softened by His Amazing grace. We endeavor to love and obey.

We have been given a wonderful family and a lot of love is shared. Our children and grandchildren are a treasure to us.

If you would like to experience His love, His forgiveness, His peace and grace, you must commit your life and ways to Jesus. Just as it was instructed to me so many years previous: Talk to Him as a friend. Forgiveness is a big thing, as He cannot forgive us until we forgive those that have hurt, offended or rejected us. Give him your heart, you will never regret this most important decision.

Pray this prayer if you like to live a life with hope and knowledge that you belong to an Amazing God who loves you and sent His Son to die for your Salvation.

"Heavenly Father, I have sinned and want to turn away from my sin and turn my face to You. Forgive me of all my wrong-doings. I believe that Jesus is the Son of God who came to this earth to save the lost by dying on the cross and I want to be found by you and have a relationship with you as my Father. Come into my heart and make me new. Fill me with your Holy Spirit so I have strength to live for you. In Jesus' name. Amen"

If you prayed this with sincerity tell someone, as the scripture says: Romans 10:9-10 *If you declare with your mouth, "Jesus is Lord," and believe in your heart that God raised him from the dead, you will be saved. 10 For it is with your heart that you believe and are justified, and it is with your mouth that you profess your faith and are saved.*

From here on in you will always belong to the winning team. Read the scriptures; it will make you strong and give you wisdom in difficult situations.

Printed in the United States
by Baker & Taylor Publisher Services